Birding Jasper National Park

Written by
KEVIN VAN TIGHEM

Drawings by
ANDREW A. LeMESSURIER

A Parks and People Publication

Copyright © Parks and People, Jasper, 1988

All rights reserved. No part of this book may be reproduced or transmitted in any form without permission in writing from the publisher, except by a reviewer, who may quote brief passages in a review.

First Edition. 1988.

Published by **Parks and People, Jasper**
under the auspices of
Jasper-Yellowhead Historical Society
in cooperation with
Canadian Parks Service
Jasper National Park
Interpretive Service

ISBN-0-921875-01-0

For additional information or copies, write to:
Parks and People, Jasper
Jasper-Yellowhead Historical Society
Box 992
Jasper, Alberta T0E 1E0

Bird and habitat drawings by Andrew A. LeMessurier
Location maps by Ann Hatfield
Design by Annette Henderson
Printed and bound in Canada by
University of Alberta Printing Services

Cover drawing: *"Willow Ptarmigan"* by Andrew A. LeMessurier

CONTENTS

ACKNOWLEDGEMENTS 1

INTRODUCTION 3

HOW TO USE THIS BOOK 7

SECTION I. FIGURING IT OUT........................... 9
  A. JASPER NATIONAL PARK: THE BASICS 10
  B. HABITATS: WHAT GROWS WHERE, AND WHY 12
    1. MONTANE LAKES AND PONDS 12
    2. MONTANE SEDGE/WILLOW WETLANDS.............. 14
    3. DOUGLAS FIR FOREST 15
    4. GRASSLANDS...................................... 15
    5. DRY SLOPES 16
    6. PINE FOREST...................................... 17
    7. FLOODPLAIN SPRUCE FOREST 18
    8. ASPEN AND BALSAM POPLAR FOREST 19
    9. MUSKEG.. 21
  10. SUBALPINE SPRUCE/FIR FOREST................... 22
  11. TIMBERLINE 23
  12. AVALANCHE SLOPES 25
  13. SHRUBLANDS.................................... 26
  14. ALPINE MEADOWS 28

SECTION II. TIMING IT RIGHT 29

SECTION III. PICKING THE PLACES 39
  A. SELECTED BIRDING DESTINATIONS 40
    1. POCAHONTAS CAMPGROUND AREA 40
    2. POCAHONTAS PONDS 41
    3. TALBOT LAKE 42
    4. MUSHROOM PATCH (Jacques Creek Fan) 44
    5. CELESTINE FIRE ROAD 45
    6. MALIGNE VALLEY ROAD 46
    7. COTTONWOOD SLOUGH 48
    8. ATHABASCA RIVER 49

9.	MIETTE VALLEY	50
10.	THE WHISTLERS and SIGNAL MOUNTAIN	52
11.	VALLEY OF FIVE LAKES	53
11.	VALLEY OF FIVE LAKES	53
12.	TONQUIN VALLEY - AMETHYST LAKES	54
13.	WILCOX PASS	55
B.	**WINTER BIRDING IN JASPER NATIONAL PARK**	56

SECTION IV. PLANNING A TRIP		57
1.	MOUNTAIN BIRD TOUR	58
2.	NORTHERN BIRD TOUR	59
3.	WESTERN BIRD TOUR	60
4.	BIG LIST BIRD TOUR	60
5.	RARITIES AND UNIQUE SPECIES BIRD TOUR	61

AFTERWORD 64

SELECTED BIBLIOGRAPHY 64

GENERAL INDEX 65

DRAWINGS

Clark's Nutcracker and Gray Jay	3
Barrow's Goldeneye	7
Female Rufous Hummingbird	9
Willow Ptarmigan	29
American Merlin	39
Boreal Owl	57

ACKNOWLEDGEMENTS

This book is a much expanded version of two earlier efforts which were entitled *"A Birder's Guide to Jasper National Park"* and *"A Checklist of the Birds of Banff and Jasper National Parks"*. The first versions were written jointly by myself and Dr. Geoff Holroyd of the Canadian Wildlife Service. At the time, I was working as a biologist on his comprehensive wildlife inventory of Jasper and Banff National Parks. I owe Geoff a special debt of gratitude for helping me to learn about Jasper's habitats and birds, encouraging me to write this guide, and being a good friend and companion on many birding trips throughout Alberta.

Another birding companion whose support, suggestions and encouragement have helped in this and many other endeavours is Gail Van Tighem: my wife. This book is dedicated to her.

The draft manuscript was reviewed and edited by Roy Richards, Jim Todgham and Andy Raniseth. Roy is recognized as one of the finest birders in Alberta; recently retired from CN Rail, he grew up in Jasper and knows the park and its birds as nobody else does. Jim Todgham has been Jasper's Chief Park Interpreter for the last decade, and Andy Raniseth is an experienced birder from Vancouver who had the good sense to move to Jasper and join the park Interpretive Service in 1986.

Without their assistance, this book would have all sorts of little glitches.

Annette Henderson, Business Manager for Parks and People, Jasper, deserves special mention since she has put a great deal of time and effort into the design and publishing of this book.

Several others have contributed to the effort to produce a comprehensive birding guide about Jasper National Park, and I appreciate all their assistance.

INTRODUCTION

Clark's Nutcracker (front) and Gray Jay

INTRODUCTION

The vast expanse of northern Rocky Mountain wilderness preserved in Jasper National Park represents many different things to people. For wildlife biologists, it is one of the world's greatest preserves of wildlife and habitat. To adventurers it offers the chance to explore a network of wilderness trails and little-known valleys. To the two million tourists who visit the park each summer, it means spectacular scenery, undisturbed wildlife, and a glimpse of what the Rockies looked like before western Canada's landscape had been rearranged by modern man.

To birders, it represents 10,878 square kilometers of almost limitless potential.

Here, where the forests and meadows of the western mountains come into contact with the muskegs and woodlands of northern Canada, where prairie-like grasslands and desert-like sand dunes can be found only a few kilometres from beaver ponds, mossy forests and alpine meadows, almost 300 species of birds have been recorded and new ones are still being discovered.

During the late 1970s and early 1980s I was fortunate enough to work on a comprehensive wildlife inventory in Jasper. It didn't take long to discover that Jasper is a place where birds typical of the prairies, the north and the western mountains all come together.

One day, while counting breeding birds on a census grid on the top of Signal Mountain, I heard something in the stunted subalpine fir, muttering, "Go back! Go back!". Forcing my way through wind-gnarled branches, I flushed a pair of willow ptarmigan. They flew a short distance, cackling with alarm, then landed and scurried back and forth, undecided whether to stay in the open and keep an eye on me, or burrow into the shintangle and hide.

A day later, on the broad mudflats of Medicine Lake, I watched a prairie falcon diving repeatedly at flocks of ruddy turnstones and semipalmated sandpipers, while Clark's nutcrackers chattered on the avalanche slopes above the road.

In Jasper you can listen to boreal owls and pygmy owls on the same evening. You can find both the eastern and the western forms of northern flicker, yellow-rumped warbler, dark-eyed junco and northern oriole (although orioles are rare). Willow ptarmigan and golden-crowned sparrows are common, yet rock wrens and prairie falcons are regularly sighted too. Roy Richards, who has lived and birded in Jasper for decades, has seen Steller's and blue jays, white-crowned, golden-crowned, white-throated and Harris' sparrows, merlin, and pygmy owl inside the Jasper townsite. In Jasper a day's list can have a little bit of everything.

The problem for the visiting birder, though, is that much of Jasper National Park is comprised of relatively unproductive coniferous forest and alpine terrain. The most interesting or productive birding areas are limited in number. To get the most out of your limited birding time, it is preferable to know in advance which areas will best meet your needs.

That's what this book is about.

HOW TO USE THIS BOOK

Barrow's Goldeneye (male)

HOW TO USE THIS BOOK

You will find no clues here on how to identify birds; there are many excellent field guides available already. This book is designed to give you tips on how to find birds.

Section I, **Figuring It Out**, helps you find the birds you want to see by understanding how the northern Rockies work. Jasper is an unfamiliar landscape to many birders who arrive here from elsewhere; this section is designed to make you feel like a native. Read it through and you'll know what habitats occur where, why they do, and what birds you can expect to find there.

Section II, **Timing It Right**, is a checklist of every species so far recorded in Jasper National Park. The bar graph beside each name shows you when that species is apt to be in the park, and how likely it is that a birder will find it. There is also a list of habitat codes that tell you where it's found.

Section III, **Picking the Places**, looks at where to find birds from the point of view of specific locations, rather than general habitats. This section highlights some of Jasper's most popular birding areas.

Section IV, **Planning a Trip**, is for birders who have a limited amount of time available, and a specific kind of birding interest.

The recommended way to use *Birding Jasper National Park*, is to go directly to Section II, select the species that interest you, and determine when your chances of finding them will be greatest. Then, using the habitat codes in the checklist, turn to Section I and look up the appropriate habitats to find out where they are, and why they occur there. Next, check Sections III and IV for suggestions on where to go, and you're all ready to hit the trail.

If you're in a hurry to find specific information, you could go directly to Sections II or III, or refer to the index.

You might find what you were looking for. You might find something new and unheard of. Either way, you'll be spending a day in one of the most spectacular and unspoiled wilderness preserves in Canada - Jasper National Park.

Section I. FIGURING IT OUT

Female Rufous Hummingbird

Section I. FIGURING IT OUT
A. JASPER NATIONAL PARK: THE BASICS

Jasper National Park encompasses 10,878 square kilometres of Rocky Mountain wilderness. It is entirely in the province of Alberta, and includes the headwaters of the Brazeau, Athabasca and Smoky Rivers. The Brazeau is a tributary of the North Saskatchewan, which flows at length to Hudson's Bay, in the Atlantic Ocean. The waters of the Athabasca and Smoky, on the other hand, reach the Arctic Ocean through the Mackenzie River system.

On a map of Jasper National Park, the eye is drawn from the icefields and glaciers of the Main Ranges on the park's western edge, down the river valleys to where they leave the Rockies. The eye is following more than just today's rivers; only a few thousand years ago those valleys held rivers of ice. The glaciers that today cling to the highest and coldest places in the Rockies once filled the valleys and covered all but the highest peaks, flowing eastwards to join the great ice sheets of the interior plains. The great glaciers retreated more than ten thousand years ago, and in fact a minor glacial advance - known as the Little Ice Age - ended barely a century and a half ago.

Most of the vegetation, birds and other wildlife that we see today became established only in the last few thousand years. The Rocky Mountain landscape is young. Changes are still taking place - for example, few people looking at the vast lodgepole pine forests of the Athabasca valley would recognize photos of the open, burned landscapes that prevailed in 1915. That's one reason why birders are still being surprised every now and then by sightings of birds not normally expected here.

Most of the vegetation of Jasper National Park is typical of the Rocky Mountains. Engelmann spruce, subalpine fir, lodgepole pine - many of the plants you see here can also be found in Colorado, Montana, British Columbia and the Yukon. So, too, can many of the typical Rocky Mountain birds like white-tailed ptarmigan, Hammond's flycatcher, water pipit, Audubon's warbler, white-crowned sparrow and rosy finch.

One of the reasons that Jasper National Park supports more ecological diversity than other mountain areas, however, is Yellowhead Pass. Like other low-elevation passes to the south, Yellowhead Pass is a gap in what is otherwise a fairly effective barrier to wind, weather and wildlife. Mild air pressing east from the Pacific Ocean squeezes through the Yellowhead Pass and is funnelled down the broad Athabasca valley, creating a long strip of vegetation which is more typical of British Columbia's montane valleys than of the high mountains. Alberta's northernmost Douglas fir forests are in the Miette and Athabasca valleys. So, too, are extensive aspen forests, dry grasslands, and a host of other productive - and rare - vegetation types. The pass also provides a corridor for British Columbia birds that favor such specialized habitats -species like Steller's jay, Lewis' woodpecker, rock wren and Say's phoebe.

The vast expanses of timberline and alpine vegetation - 40% of Jasper National Park is above the tree line - seem to have allowed some characteristic birds of arctic Canada to extend their ranges south into the park. Willow ptarmigan and golden-crowned sparrows are fairly common. Baird's sandpiper is sometimes seen in alpine meadows in July, although it doesn't appear to breed here. Even grey-cheeked thrushes have been found at timberline in the breeding season.

One more element of diversity is worth mentioning: the boreal influence that extends into Jasper National Park along the Athabasca valley. Unlike the rivers that drain Banff National Park and the southern Canadian Rockies, the Athabasca River swings north and east through a region of northern forest. Boreal forests of black spruce and tamarack, typical of Canada's north, followed the retreating glaciers back into the Rockies and have brought with them several unique bird species. Greater yellowlegs, ovenbird, Leconte's sparrow and white-throated sparrow are among boreal species that breed in Jasper but are rare farther south in the Rockies.

So Jasper is really at a crossroads between north and south and between east and west. It is a dynamic environment, still sorting itself out after the last ice age; changes in bird populations can be seen from one year to the next. A severe winter storm in northern Alberta, strong westerly winds sweeping inland from the Pacific, a late spring on the prairies - there are many influences that can send rare wanderers into Jasper's sheltered valleys or lead to a sudden change in distribution or concentration of breeding birds.

A friend of mine calls it the "random factor". It's what makes birding Jasper National Park so exciting: not only are you likely to see birds you aren't used to seeing at home, but there's also a chance of seeing such unexpected rarities as black-legged kittiwake, parasitic jaeger, western kingbird or swamp sparrow - all of which have been seen in Jasper.

B. HABITATS: WHAT GROWS WHERE, AND WHY

The key to successful birding is to understand where the birds you seek live, and why they are there. In fact, the key to really enjoying any kind of activity in an unfamiliar area is to understand your surroundings. Habitat itself is as fascinating as the animals that use it, and considerably more important. After all, animals that die may eventually be replaced by others, but if their habitat is gone they can never return.

This section will help you to understand the different habitats that together comprise the mosaic of scenic beauty and wildlife wealth that we know as the northern Rocky Mountains. Given the size of this birders' guide, the descriptions have to be fairly short. For more information, consult the books listed on page 64.

Starting at the valley-bottom and working up to the summits, the following comprise the typical habitats of Jasper National Park:

1. MONTANE LAKES AND PONDS

Although lakes and ponds are scarce in the Rocky Mountains as a whole, in Jasper National Park there are several waterbodies, mostly along the Miette and Athabasca valleys.

The immense glaciers that carved these valleys widened and flattened the valley floors. In places where softer rock was exposed, the ice carved long grooves. In some places the glaciers left dams of rock rubble at the ends of deep hollows. In still other places, huge blocks of stagnant ice remained trapped in the gravelly debris left by the retreating glaciers; when these chunks melted they formed rounded kettle ponds. Lakes and ponds formed by all of these processes can be seen within a few kilometres of Jasper townsite.

Other montane ponds are formed by beavers, damming small streams such as Cottonwood and Wabasso Creeks. And some of the most productive wetlands are on the floodplain of the Miette and Athabasca Rivers, where spring floods overflow the river banks and deposit water and silt on adjacent flat areas each year.

The productivity of these wet areas is generally low, at least so far as waterfowl and shorebirds are concerned. Most of the lakes on the Pyramid bench, behind Jasper townsite, support a pair of loons, one or two families of Barrow's goldeneye, and a few non-breeding teal or mallards. The larger lakes, like Patricia and Pyramid, Edith and Annette, support scoters, red-necked grebes, lesser scaup and ring-necked ducks, but they still lack the high bird densities of lakes on the prairies and other areas. Because they are cold and low in nutrients, they produce little vegetation and little aquatic life, and consequently don't support a lot of ducks.

The most productive ponds in the Jasper townsite area are Cottonwood Slough and Mildred Lake. Farther east, Talbot Lake and Pocahontas ponds are worth a visit. Ospreys are regularly seen around most lakes, and nest at Pyramid, Patricia, Cabin, Talbot and other lakes in the area.

2. MONTANE SEDGE/WILLOW WETLANDS

The edges of lakes and ponds, beaverpond areas and the floodplains of the larger rivers and streams are much more productive than the wetlands themselves. Here, water-loving vegetation like willows, sedges, black spruce and poplar provide a variety of habitats for numerous species of birds. It is a well known fact that the more diverse the vegetation, the more diverse and abundant the wildlife. In the ridged landscapes of the Pyramid Bench and the Valley of Five Lakes area, forest and grassland alternate with sedge/willow wetlands along creeks and lake edges; these are excellent birding areas.

Among the most productive wetland areas are Pocahontas Ponds, the Mushroom Patch, Cottonwood Slough, and the Wabasso Creek beaverponds along the Valley of Five Lakes trail.

During the breeding season common snipes winnow overhead while alder flycatchers and - less commonly - willow flycatchers call from the shrubbery. Song and Lincoln's sparrows, yellow, Wilson's and Tennessee warblers, northern yellowthroats, red-winged blackbirds and ruby-crowned kinglets sing in the willows and forest edges. Rufous hummingbirds are common, as are violet-green and tree swallows. An early morning visit to a beaverpond or floodplain complex can be almost overwhelming; these areas support by far the greatest density and diversity of bird life in the park.

3. DOUGLAS FIR FOREST

By contrast, Douglas fir forest is generally quiet and peaceful. The huge old trees, with their sparse undergrowth, provide a simple habitat that supports fewer bird species.

Nonetheless, it is worth spending time in Jasper's Douglas fir forest. It's a rare habitat in Alberta's Rockies, limited to sunny, south-facing slopes at low elevations. This habitat is much more common in British Columbia and the western U.S.A., and is among the few places in Jasper where birders can find such western species as western tanager, Cassin's finch, pygmy owl, mountain chickadee and - rarely - Lewis' woodpecker. Other regularly sighted birds include red-breasted nuthatch, northern flicker, pileated woodpecker and American kestrel.

4. GRASSLANDS

There are very few places left in the Rocky Mountains where you can watch birds and other wildlife in undisturbed grassland. Banff National Park lost most of its grasslands to a boundary revision in 1930. The beautiful and historic Kootenay Plains along the North

Saskatchewan River were largely flooded when the Bighorn Dam was built in the late 1960s. But in Jasper National Park, extensive natural grasslands can be found along the Athabasca valley from Jasper townsite to the east park entrance.

While Jasper's grasslands are critical to the survival of elk, bighorn sheep and other large mammals, they do not support a great variety of bird life. Vesper sparrow, common nighthawk, American kestrel and western meadowlark are among the few species more common in the montane grasslands than elsewhere.

Old-timers recall when mountain bluebirds were also fairly common along the grassland edges, but they are seen now mainly on migration. Whether the current abundance of European starlings accounts for the absence of bluebirds, or whether pesticide use in wintering areas or some other factor is involved, it is sadly obvious that even the protected world of a national park can be affected by the way we misuse land and wildlife, even when the damage takes place far away from the parks.

5. DRY SLOPES

Along the wind-blown Athabasca valley, and in many parts of the Front Ranges, south facing slopes are dry and open. Not only do these slopes get much more exposure to sunshine than do others, but they are frequently swept by drying winds. The coarse veneer of glacial gravels and moraine does not hold moisture well, and soil forms slowly.

The resulting habitat is a special one, appreciated not only by bighorn sheep, mule deer and golden-mantled ground squirrels, but by a number of bird species as well. Some dry slopes are carpeted by bearberry and tussocks of grass. Others have clumps of white spruce, Douglas fir or even lodgepole pine. In most places, trees grow in gullies or downhill from rock outcrops while sparse groundcover carpets the more exposed areas.

This type of habitat is common along the Celestine Road and near Disaster Point, above the Yellowhead highway. Hikers can spend time on open slopes along the Sulphur Skyline trail or some of the trails near Jasper townsite.

Characteristic species found in this habitat include northern goshawk, American kestrel, blue grouse, pygmy owl, calliope hummingbird, Clark's nutcracker, Townsend's solitaire, and chipping sparrow. These are also likely spots to watch for such rarities as Say's phoebe, Lewis' woodpecker and rock wren.

6. PINE FOREST

Pine forest is one of the most widespread, and least interesting, habitats in Jasper National Park. Early prospectors sometimes burned off huge tracts of land just to see the underlying rock strata or to make travel easier. Early explorers and travellers set fires accidentally. Sparks from steam engines on the railways regularly set the surrounding forests on fire. There were very few tracts of low elevation forest left unburned by the time Jasper National Park's boundaries were finally set in the 1930 National Parks Act.

More than half a century of careful fire protection has passed since, and even-aged forests of lodgepole pine have grown back in the burned areas.

Lodgepole pine is self-pruning; that is, since its needles need lots of sunshine to survive, the lower branches die as the tree grows older. Mature pines have a clump of foliage at the top, and a long, branchless trunk. The forest floor is usually sparsely vegetated, with scattered buffaloberry or juniper shrubs and a little ryegrass or bearberry.

In so simple a habitat, and one which provides so little useful shelter, only a few of the more common bird species can do well. Hammond's flycatcher, gray jay, boreal chickadee, American robin, Swainson's thrush, yellow-rumped warbler, solitary vireo, and chipping sparrow are the most common species. If the pine forest is mixed with aspen or spruce, and if the understory is diverse or there is a lot of dead and dying timber, however, the stand may be worth exploring. Mixed forest with old pines is a very productive habitat, providing food and shelter both for species typical of deciduous woods and for those of coniferous stands.

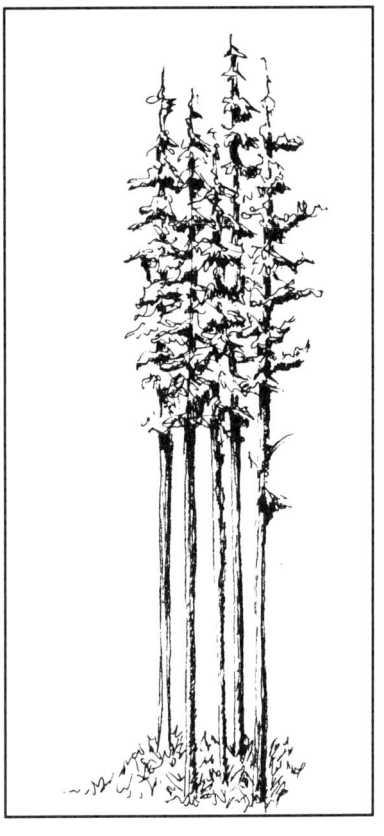

7. FLOODPLAIN SPRUCE FOREST

In addition to the sparse white spruce cover on dry slopes, and the black spruce forest of wetland areas, there are a few fairly extensive groves of white spruce along streams and rivers at low elevations. Some good stands can be seen near the Mushroom Patch and along the lower Miette valley. These spruce forests are generally associated with balsam poplar and sedge/willow areas, so it is hard to separate out the bird species that are dependent on the spruce from those found there because of the diverse associated vegetation.

These trees are often quite old. Possibly because they grow in floodplain areas where the soil is moist and there is occasional flooding, some of these forest stands survived the big fires around the turn of the century. A land surveyor named Bridgland photographed most of Jasper's front country in 1915; his photos show an almost prairie-like landscape with strips of dark spruce timber along the Miette River and in other areas.

Old trees tend to get sick, and sick trees tend to rot. Because of this, the old-growth forests along the Miette and Athabasca Rivers are extremely valuable woodpecker and owl habitats. The insect-infested trees provide abundant food for three-toed, pileated, downy and hairy woodpeckers, as well as both the red and yellow-shafted forms of the northern flicker. Abandoned nest holes of the various woodpeckers provide nest sites for saw-whet, boreal and pygmy owls. Barred owls are regularly recorded along the lower Miette valley and in other old-growth floodplain forests.

Tennessee warbler, Wilson's warbler, rufous hummingbird and western tanager are among a variety of other species that inhabit floodplain spruce stands, especially along the forest edges. One of the most fascinating May or June birding trips in Jasper can be a quiet canoe trip down the Miette River from the highway bridge two km west of Jasper townsite through groves of huge old white spruce and balsam poplars and a mosaic of other wetland habitats.

8. ASPEN AND BALSAM POPLAR FOREST

There are some beautiful stands of aspen and balsam poplar within easy reach of Jasper townsite. Aspen forest in Jasper National Park is one good example of how something can seem more common than it really is, simply because it is accessible. In all the thousands of square kilometres of Rocky Mountain wilderness preserved within Jasper's boundaries, only the lower Miette and Athabasca valleys and small parts of other Front Range valleys have aspen forest.

Aspen grows in well-drained soil in areas with a reasonably long growing season. In the Rockies, this means either in the lowest, warmest valleys, or on south-facing slopes at low elevations. These are the same areas that humans like to develop, so it is little wonder that our roads and facilities are often in and near aspen forests.

Aspen forest is also a valuable wildlife habitat. Deer, elk, black bear and other large animals rely on aspens for food and shelter; so, too, do a number of scarce bird species.

One thing about aspens and other deciduous trees that make them important to hole-nesting birds like woodpeckers, chickadees, bluebirds and others, is that the trees generally only live 50 to 75 years. Because the inner wood dies as the tree grows, leaving a ring of healthy growing wood around a core of dying or rotting inner wood, the trees are ideal for hole-digging birds.

In addition, aspen forests are sunny places, with a diversity of vegetation and cover. Insects are abundant and food is available for many birds that would waste away to nothing if forced to forage in the gloom of a coniferous forest.

So it's worthwhile for a birder to wander about on the trails that start near Patricia and Pyramid Lakes and Cottonwood Slough, or to stop in some of the aspen and balsam poplar groves along the Celestine Road. These are good places to look for such species as red-tailed hawk, ruffed grouse, saw-whet owl, yellow-bellied sapsucker, least flycatcher, western wood pewee, hermit thrush, warbling vireo, orange-crowned warbler, purple finch, pine siskin and chipping sparrow.

9. MUSKEG

To really appreciate muskeg you have to read the journals of early travellers like Milton and Cheadle, Mary Schäffer and others who visited Jasper in the 1800s and early 1900s - without the benefit of roads. Paved highways tend to give us an unrealistic view of the landscape. A day of foot travel through muskegs and over rocky ridges is good for the soul; it brings us back down to earth so to speak. It's also the only way to find some of Jasper's more interesting birdlife.

Muskeg is any poorly drained area where sphagnum and other mosses, or sedges, build up a thick layer of spongy, water-soaked peat. In some places, a mat of peat grows out and covers over part or all of a small pond so that the unwary traveller can break right through into the black gumbo underneath. The ground is generally hummocky, with dwarf birch or labrador tea growing on the moss hummocks, and with scattered clumps of black spruce.

Muskeg produces moose, moss and mosquitoes. Take your insect repellant. It also produces ruby-crowned kinglet, blackpoll warbler, olive-sided flycatcher, common snipe, savannah and Lincoln's sparrows, Hammond's and alder flycatchers, and dark-eyed junco. Spruce grouse like the heavily wooded edges of muskegs, and rarities such as the palm or magnolia warbler may occasionally turn up.

There are areas of muskeg near Cottonwood Slough and Riley Lake, around Honeymoon Lake, at the north end of Talbot Lake, and just north of the Sunwapta District Warden Station near the Columbia Icefield area. An hour of slogging around, slapping mosquitos and discovering long-forgotten muscles may produce some unusual bird sightings and will certainly make you appreciate dry ground again.

10. SUBALPINE SPRUCE/FIR FOREST

The higher you ascend in the Rocky Mountains, the more likely you are to find yourself in spruce/fir forest rather than the ubiquitous pine forests of the low valleys. At higher elevations the summers are cooler, the winters snowier, and the drought conditions that lead to forest fires occur less often. Some of Jasper National Park's oldest trees are in the high-elevation forests near the Athabasca Glacier.

Spruce/fir forest is generally unproductive for birds. Unlike pines, these trees keep their lower branches as they age, so that very little sunlight reaches the forest floor. Mosses and spindly shrubs like menziesia or rhododendron are among the sparse understory vegetation, and deciduous trees are very rare.

Many of Jasper National Park's hiking trails wander through the subalpine spruce/fir forests. Some examples include the Cavell meadows trail, the Watchtower trail and the Tonquin Valley trail. Here you will find Hammond's flycatcher, Clark's nutcracker, boreal chickadee, red-breasted nuthatch, winter wren, varied thrush, hermit and swainson's thrushes, golden-crowned kinglet, Townsend's and Wilson's warblers and Oregon junco.

11. TIMBERLINE

Even on the sunniest summer day, you are unlikely to trip over a sun-bather on the summit of The Whistlers or any of Jasper National Park's other accessible mountains. It's just too cold up there. The higher you go, the thinner the air gets, and thin air holds little heat. As a result, you can get a fine sunburn on top of a mountain, but you'll rarely be too warm.

Not only is the air cooler at high elevations, but summer is shorter, winds are stronger, and life is just generally more difficult for anything that grows more than a few inches above the ground. At about 2100 m, timberline marks the zone where the alpine climate becomes too severe for trees. Above that elevation, vegetation is restricted to grasses, heaths and other small plants that take shelter close to the ground.

In some places, timberline is abrupt. Elsewhere, though, it covers a broad band along the mountain slope. The heavy spruce/fir canopy of the middle slopes begins to open up with small meadows of scrub willow, grass and forbs, or heather. Higher up, the meadows become larger, and higher yet the forest is reduced to islands of stunted trees. At the very upper limits of tree growth, the trees are little more than windblown shrubs, called krummholz or shintangle, sprawled flat along the ground.

Because of its mix of forest and meadow habitats, and the resulting diversity of feeding and shelter areas, timberline supports higher densities and diversity of bird life than either the forest below or the alpine meadows above. A walk to the Cavell meadows or along the Skyline Trail or Wilcox Pass trail will usually produce such typical timberline species as rufous hummingbird, northern flicker, Clark's nutcracker, American robin, varied thrush, mountain bluebird, Townsend's solitaire, ruby-crowned kinglet, water pipit,

Wilson's warbler, pine grosbeak, white-crowned and golden-crowned sparrows, fox sparrow and, in some areas, willow ptarmigan and Brewer's sparrow. Because rodents like the hoary marmot and Columbian ground squirrel are common at timberline, this is also a good spot to watch for golden eagles.

12. AVALANCHE SLOPES

Avalanche slopes are not - for obvious reasons - recommended for winter birding, but they can be excellent places to explore in June and July. Snow builds up each winter, especially on the northeast (lee) sides of mountains. In some locations it becomes unstable, eventually collapses, and slides down the slope, coming to rest at the base of the mountainside. The slides vary in size from year to year, but over the years they tend to keep the forest at bay, breaking off any trees rash enough to poke their heads above the protective snowpack.

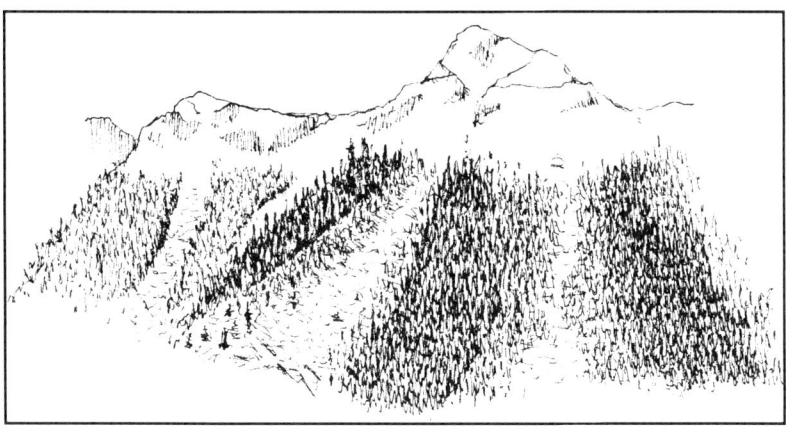

Since trees cannot survive the annual pounding of snow avalanches, other vegetation grows on avalanche tracks instead. Alder and willow, low flexible shrubs that can bend before the on-rushing snow, are common. Patches of stunted subalpine fir, meadows of tall grasses and forbs, berry-producing shrubs like huckleberry and currant: avalanche slopes are usually a patchwork quilt of lush vegetation. They are important summer feeding areas for elk, moose, grizzly bears and other animals, and produce a diversity of birds.

Most of Jasper's longer trails cross avalanche slopes at some point. The Portal Creek trail into the Tonquin Valley, and the Geraldine Lakes trail are two that give easy access to avalanche slopes. The trail to the summit of The Whistlers starts in a former ski area that has many of the characteristics of an avalanche slope.

Many of the birds found at timberline or on dry open slopes also occur on avalanche slopes. In addition, you can often find boreal owl, three-toed woodpecker, Hammond's flycatcher, olive-sided flycatcher, red-breasted nuthatch, Townsend's, Wilson's and MacGillivray's warblers, and Lincoln's sparrow.

13. SHRUBLANDS

In the extensive coniferous forests of the Rocky Mountains, it is the openings that produce habitat and wildlife diversity. Timberline and avalanche slopes are among the few places where the forest canopy opens up. Another such place is the cold-air drainage pockets along high elevation valleys.

You may have already noticed, if you arrived in Jasper after having driven the Icefields Parkway from Banff, that the high valleys have both an upper and a lower timberline. The spruce/fir forest is a fringe of timber separating alpine meadows from broad, valley-bottom meadows.

The shrubby meadows along stream valleys in the Rockies are the result of a couple of things. On the one hand, the soil is poorly drained in many valley bottoms, and trees find it difficult to grow well because of the wet, boggy soil. In addition, since cold air is heavy and tends to drain downslope and pool in hollows like water, the valley bottoms are frost pockets, where cold air drainage results in a greater frequency of frosty nights than higher on the slopes. Trees need more frost-free hours each year to grow and thrive than are available in these cold air drainage areas.

These shrub meadows are covered with scrub willow and dwarf birch, grass and sedge stands, and occasional clumps of spruce.

The streams that wind through the meadows are dammed by beavers in some areas.

One of the most accessible areas of this sort is in Sunwapta Pass, right at the Jasper/Banff boundary. Other places where you can find productive shrublands include the Opal Hills trail near Maligne Lake, the Tonquin Valley, and parts of the Skyline Trail.

Watch for many of the common timberline or avalanche slope species. In addition, you may find harlequin duck, spotted sandpiper, common snipe, alder flycatcher, barn swallow, American dipper, Bohemian waxwing and savannah sparrow. During late August and September, these meadows are good spots to watch for migrating golden eagles and northern harriers.

14. ALPINE MEADOWS

Alpine meadows are a lot less common than might be expected. What many people refer to as alpine is really more typical of timberline. True alpine is the land above the last trees, a land of rock, talus and low-growing vegetation. In Jasper, the most accessible alpine areas are the summit of The Whistlers and the Cavell meadows. There are also extensive alpine meadows on Signal Mountain, in Wilcox Pass, and at Maccarib Pass on the Tonquin Valley trail.

Alpine meadows support a low density of birds, but the surroundings are spectacular, the birds are highly visible, and many of the species that occur there may not be found elsewhere. Among characteristic alpine species in Jasper National Park are white-tailed ptarmigan, water pipit, horned lark and rosy finch.

Section II. TIMING IT RIGHT

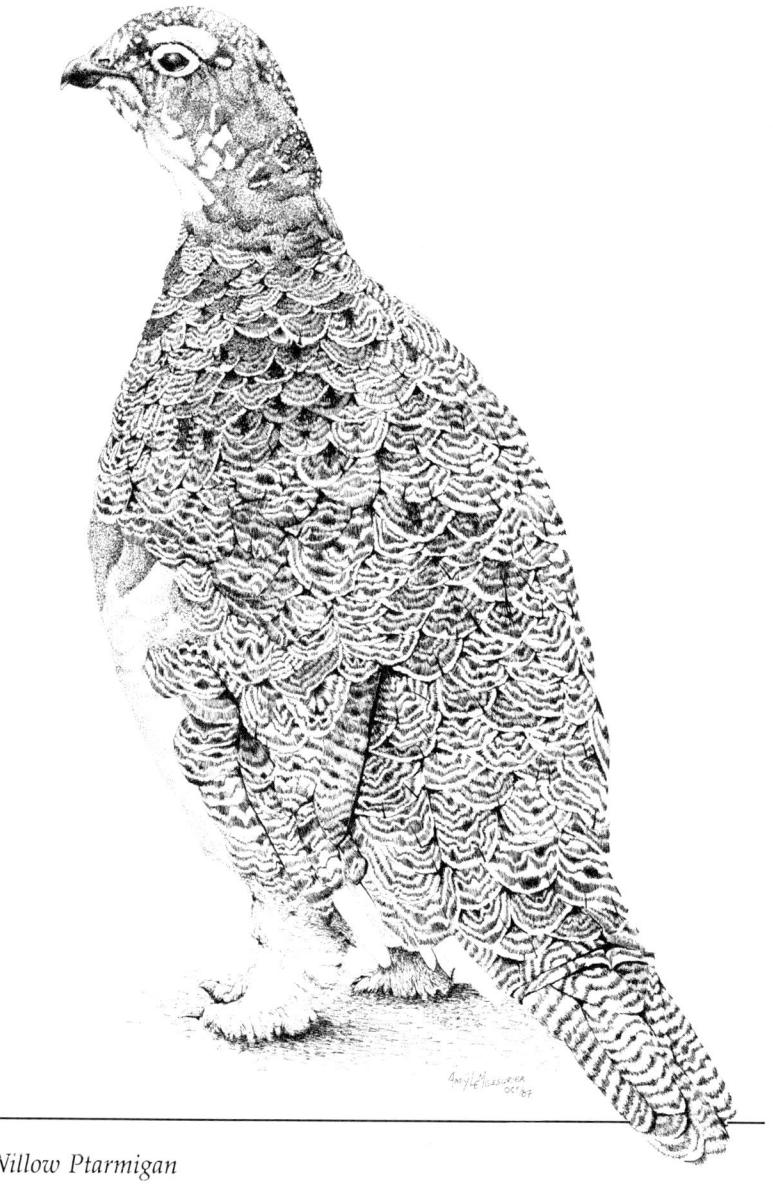

Willow Ptarmigan

Section II. TIMING IT RIGHT
ANNOTATED CHECKLIST OF THE BIRDS OF JASPER NATIONAL PARK

LEGEND

HABITAT CODES

- C   Coniferous forest
- P   Pine forest
- S   Spruce forest
- F   Douglas fir forest
- B   Burned areas
- D   Deciduous forest
- G   Grassland
- L   Lakes and ponds
- R   Rivers
- W   Wetland areas (willow & sedge)
- M   Shrub meadows
- Y   Muskeg
- O   Open dry slopes
- X   Avalanche slopes
- K   Timberline
- A   Alpine areas
- T   Townsites, landfills, etc.

SEASONAL ABUNDANCE

In one day a competent birder in appropriate habitat might expect to find the following numbers of individuals of each species:

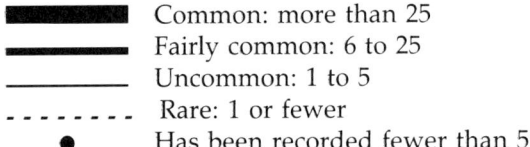

- Common: more than 25
- Fairly common: 6 to 25
- Uncommon: 1 to 5
- Rare: 1 or fewer
- ● Has been recorded fewer than 5 times.

BREEDING STATUS

*   An asterisk indicates species having bred in Jasper, or regularly seen in breeding season.

	HABITAT CODE	MONTH J F M A M J J A S O N D
— Pacific Loon	L	
— Common Loon*	L	
— Pied-billed Grebe*	L,W	
— Horned Grebe	L,W	
— Red-necked Grebe*	L,W	
— Eared Grebe	L,W	
— Western Grebe	L,W	
— American White Pelican	L	
— Double-crested Cormorant	L	
— American Bittern*	L,W	
— Great Blue Heron	L,R,W	
— Tundra Swan	L,R	
— Trumpeter Swan	L,R	
— Snow Goose	L	
— Brant	L	
— Canada Goose*	L,R,W	
— Wood Duck	W	
— Green-winged Teal*	L,R,W	
— Mallard*	L,R,W	
— Pintail*	L,R,W	
— Blue-winged Teal*	L,R,W	
— Cinnamon Teal	L,R,W	
— Northern Shoveler	L,R,W	
— Gadwall	L,R,W	
— Eurasian Wigeon	L,R,W	
— American Wigeon*	L,R,W	
— Canvasback	L,W	
— Redhead	L,W	
— Ring-necked Duck*	L,R,W	
— Greater Scaup	L,R,W	
— Lesser Scaup*	L,R,W	
— Harlequin Duck*	L,R	

	HABITAT CODE	MONTH J F M A M J J A S O N D
— Oldsquaw	L	
— Surf Scoter	L	
— White-winged Scoter	L	
— Common Goldeneye	L,R,W	
— Barrow's Goldeneye*	L,R,W	
— Bufflehead*	L,R,W	
— Hooded Merganser	L,R,W	
— Common Merganser*	L,R	
— Red-breasted Merganser	L,R	
— Ruddy Duck	L,R,W	
— Osprey*	L,R,W	
— Bald Eagle*	L,R,W	
— Northern Harrier	W,M,G	
— Sharp-shinned Hawk*	C,D,O,X	
— Cooper's Hawk*	C,D,O,X	
— Northern Goshawk*	C,D,O,X	
— Red-tailed Hawk*	C,D,G,M,O	
— Ferruginous Hawk	G,O	
— Rough-legged Hawk	G,M,W	
— Golden Eagle*	A,K,O,M	
— American Kestrel*	O,X,M,G,B	
— Merlin*	C,D,O	
— Peregrine Falcon	L,R,W,O	
— Gyrfalcon	A,G,M	
— Prairie Falcon	O,A,M,L,G	
— Gray Partridge	T,G	
— Spruce Grouse*	S,P,Y	
— Blue Grouse*	O,K,X,B	
— Willow Ptarmigan*	K,X,M	
— White-tailed Ptarmigan*	A,K,X,M	
— Ruffed Grouse*	D,F,S	
— Sharp-tailed Grouse	M,W,G	

	HABITAT CODE	MONTH J F M A M J J A S O N D
— Yellow Rail	W	
— Sora*	W	
— American Coot	W,L	
— Sandhill Crane	L,W,R	
— Black-bellied Plover	L,R	
— Lesser Golden-Plover	L,R	
— Semipalmated Plover	L,R	
— Killdeer*	L,R,G,W	
— Greater Yellowlegs*	L,R,W,Y	
— Lesser Yellowlegs	L,R,W,Y	
— Solitary Sandpiper*	L,R,W,Y	
— Wandering Tattler	L	
— Spotted Sandpiper*	L,R,W,Y	
— Upland Sandpiper	G,M,T	
— Eskimo Curlew	M,W	
— Sanderling	L,R	
— Semipalmated Sandpiper	L,R	
— Western Sandpiper	L,R	
— Least Sandpiper	L,R	
— Baird's Sandpiper	L,R,W	
— Pectoral Sandpiper	L,R,W	
— Dunlin	L,R	
— Stilt Sandpiper	L,W	
— Buff-breasted Sandpiper	L,W	
— Long-billed Dowitcher	L,R,W,Y	
— Common Snipe*	W,Y,M	
— Wilson's Phalarope	W,L	
— Red-necked Phalarope	L,R,W	
— Parasitic Jaeger	W,M	
— Long-tailed Jaeger	T,L	
— Franklin's Gull	L,R,T	
— Bonaparte's Gull	L,R	

	HABITAT CODE	J F M A M J J A S O N D
__ Sabine's Gull	L,R	
__ Mew Gull	L,R,T	
__ Ring-billed Gull	L,R,T	
__ California Gull	L,R,T	
__ Herring Gull	L,R,T	
__ Thayer's Gull	L,R,T	
__ Black-legged Kittiwake	L	
__ Common Tern	L,R,W	
__ Forster's Tern	L,R,W	
__ Black Tern	L,W,R	
__ Band-tailed Pigeon	O,F	
__ Rock Dove*	T	
__ Mourning Dove*	O,F,D	
__ Great Horned Owl*	S,F,D	
__ Snowy Owl	G,L,W	
__ Northern Hawk-Owl*	Y,B,K	
__ Northern Pygmy-Owl*	F,O	
__ Burrowing Owl	T	
__ Barred Owl*	F,D,S	
__ Great Gray Owl	D,Y	
__ Short-eared Owl	M	
__ Boreal Owl*	P,S,Y	
__ Northern Saw-whet Owl*	D,O,S,W	
__ Common Nighthawk*	O,G,T	
__ Black Swift*	R	
__ Ruby-throated Hummingbird	T	
__ Calliope Hummingbird*	T,B,O,W	
__ Rufous Hummingbird*	T,W,B,X,P	
__ Belted Kingfisher*	R,L	
__ Lewis' Woodpecker*	B,O,F	
__ Yellow-bellied Sapsucker*	D	
__ Red-naped Sapsucker	D	

	HABITAT CODE	MONTH J F M A M J J A S O N D
— Downy Woodpecker*	D,W,T	
— Hairy Woodpecker*	D,C,O,T,W	
— Three-toed Woodpecker*	S,P,B	
— Black-backed Woodpecker	B,O,T	
— Northern Flicker*	O,F,B,G,D	
— Pileated Woodpecker*	F,D,O	
— Olive-sided Flycatcher*	Y,X,B,O	
— Western Wood-Pewee*	D,W	
— Alder Flycatcher*	W,M,X	
— Willow Flycatcher*	W	
— Least Flycatcher*	D	
— Hammond's Flycatcher*	C,D	
— Dusky Flycatcher*	O,D,X	
— Western Flycatcher*	P,D,R	
— Eastern Phoebe	W,T,R	
— Say's Phoebe	O,T	
— Western Kingbird	T,G	
— Eastern Kingbird*	W	
— Horned Lark*	A	
— Tree Swallow*	W,T,L	
— Violet-green Swallow*	W,T,L	
— N. Rough-winged Swallow*	W,L,R	
— Bank Swallow*	W,L,R	
— Cliff Swallow*	L,R	
— Barn Swallow*	L,R,T,W,M	
— Gray Jay*	C,T	
— Steller's Jay	C,T	
— Blue Jay	T	
— Clark's Nutcracker*	O,X,K,F,T	
— Black-billed Magpie*	G,P,T	
— American Crow*	G,P,T,D,F	
— Common Raven*	G,C,D,M,T	

	HABITAT CODE	MONTH J F M A M J J A S O N D
— Black-capped Chickadee*	D,W,T	
— Mountain Chickadee*	F,O,T,P,K	
— Boreal Chickadee*	C,T	
— Red-breasted Nuthatch*	C,T	
— Pygmy Nuthatch	O,F	
— Brown Creeper*	F,S,D	
— Rock Wren	O	
— House Wren	W,D	
— Winter Wren*	S,X,K	
— Marsh Wren	W	
— American Dipper*	R,L	
— Golden-crowned Kinglet*	S,F,P	
— Ruby-crowned Kinglet*	Y,X,S,C,R	
— Mountain Bluebird*	K,M,O,B,G	
— Townsend's Solitaire*	X,K,O	
— Gray-cheeked Thrush	K	
— Swainson's Thrush*	S,P,F	
— Hermit Thrush*	K,P,F,D,S	
— American Robin*	K,C,D,T	
— Varied Thrush*	S,F,K,X	
— Gray Catbird	D	
— Brown Thrasher	D,T	
— Bendire's Thrasher	G	
— Water Pipit*	A,L,R	
— Bohemian Waxwing*	Y,W,O,T	
— Cedar Waxwing*	W,D,T	
— Northern Shrike	W,G	
— European Starling*	C,D,T,B	
— Solitary Vireo*	F,P,D	
— Warbling Vireo*	D,W,T	
— Philadelphia Vireo	P	
— Red-eyed Vireo*	D,S	

	HABITAT CODE	J F M A M J J A S O N D
— Tennessee Warbler*	W,Y,S,D	
— Orange-crowned Warbler*	W,D	
— Yellow Warbler*	W	
— Magnolia Warbler	S,Y	
— Cape May Warbler	S	
— Yellow-rumped Warbler*	C,T,Y	
— Townsend's Warbler*	S,F,X	
— Palm Warbler	Y	
— Bay-breasted Warbler	S	
— Blackpoll Warbler*	Y,S,W	
— American Redstart*	W	
— Ovenbird*	D	
— Northern Waterthrush*	W,Y	
— MacGillivray's Warbler*	X,W,M	
— Common Yellowthroat*	W,M	
— Wilson's Warbler*	W,S,Y,X,K	
— Canada Warbler	C	
— Western Tanager*	F,P,D	
— Rose-breasted Grosbeak	D	
— Black-headed Grosbeak	D,S	
— Lazuli Bunting	O,D,B	
— Rufous-sided Towhee	T	
— American Tree Sparrow	W,M,D,T	
— Chipping Sparrow*	F,K,T	
— Clay-colored Sparrow*	M,W	
— Brewer's Sparrow*	K,M	
— Vesper Sparrow*	G,O	
— Savannah Sparrow*	W,M,Y	
— LeConte's Sparrow*	W	
— Fox Sparrow*	K,X,W	
— Song Sparrow*	W	
— Lincoln's Sparrow*	W,M,Y	

Species	HABITAT CODE	J	F	M	A	M	J	J	A	S	O	N	D
— Swamp Sparrow	W			●	●					●			
— White-throated Sparrow*	W,S,D	●								●	●	●	●
— Golden-crowned Sparrow*	K,S												
— White-crowned Sparrow*	S,W,R,Y		●										●
— Harris' Sparrow	T												
— Dark-eyed Junco*	C,D,T,K,B	●											
— Lapland Longspur	G				●				●			●	●
— Chestnut-collared Longspur	G				●								
— Snow Bunting	G,W,L,O				●								
— Red-winged Blackbird*	W,L,S									●	●	●	●
— Western Meadowlark	G			●		●				●	●		
— Yellow-headed Blackbird	W,T						●	●		●	●		
— Rusty Blackbird*	W,Y,T												
— Brewer's Blackbird*	W,M,T	●										●	●
— Common Grackle	T					●	●	●		●			
— Brown-headed Cowbird*	D,M,W,T,C										●	●	
— Northern Oriole	D						●	●					
— Rosy Finch*	A,K,X												
— Pine Grosbeak*	O,C,X,T												
— Purple Finch*	D,T												
— Cassin's Finch	F,T					●	●			●			
— House Finch	T					●	●						
— Red Crossbill*	C												
— White-winged Crossbill*	C												
— Hoary Redpoll	W,T,D,X				●								●
— Common Redpoll	W,T,D,X					●		●			●		
— American Goldfinch	D,G,T					●							
— Pine Siskin*	C,M,T												
— Evening Grosbeak*	C,T												
— House Sparrow*	T												

38

Section III. PICKING THE PLACES

Young American Merlin

Section III. PICKING THE PLACES
A. SELECTED BIRDING DESTINATIONS

Depending on habitat, access and other factors, some places are better than others for finding birds. The following list includes Jasper National Park's most popular birding spots. It is not intended to imply that other places in Jasper National Park may not be equally productive or even more rewarding, but the areas listed here are both accessible and representative in terms of Jasper's habitats and birds. Species lists are not intended to be comprehensive.

1. POCAHONTAS CAMPGROUND AREA

Location: Four kilometres up the Fiddle valley road from the junction with highway 16 at Pocahontas, which is 8.5 km from the Jasper east gateway.

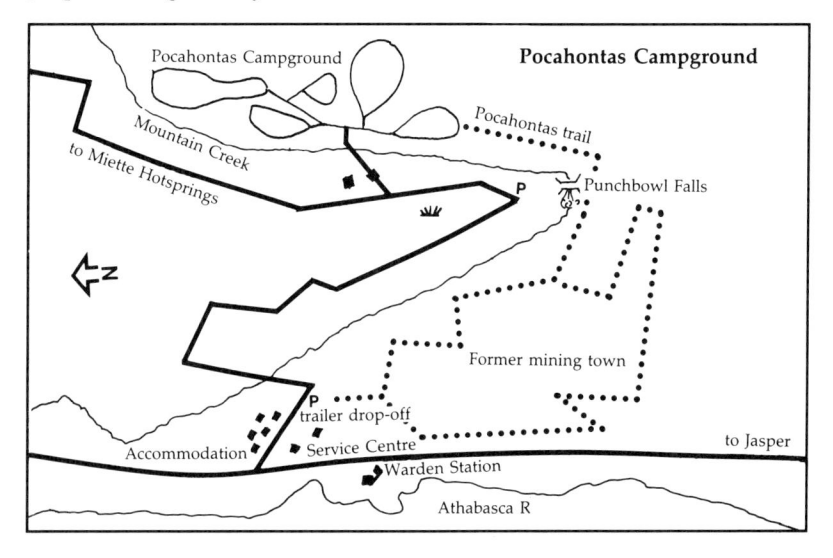

Pocahontas Campground

Habitat: Mixed forest of white spruce, lodgepole pine, balsam poplar and aspen, with a fairly lush understory, especially in more open areas. Montane life zone, but with a lot of plants and some birds more typical of the boreal life zone.

Birding: The campground is normally open only from mid-May until the beginning of September.

> *May*: An excellent area to watch for boreal warblers and sparrows on migration. The best period is during the last ten days of the month. You will almost certainly find ovenbird and white-throated sparrow.
>
> *June to mid-July:* The diverse vegetation creates an ideal habitat for several species. Take a half-day hike from the campground to the old mining town of Pocahontas (ask at the kiosk for directions to the trail) and you will find spruce forest, mixed forest, open dry hillsides, balsam poplar forest, alder thickets and disturbed areas - a mixture that should produce rufous hummingbird, least and Hammond's flycatchers, solitary vireo, warbling vireo, Tennessee warbler, blackpoll warbler, ovenbird, clay-colored sparrow, and white-throated sparrow.

2. POCAHONTAS PONDS

Location: North side of highway 16, 8.8 km from the Jasper east gateway. Parking is available at the service centre on the south side of the highway, 1/4 km east.

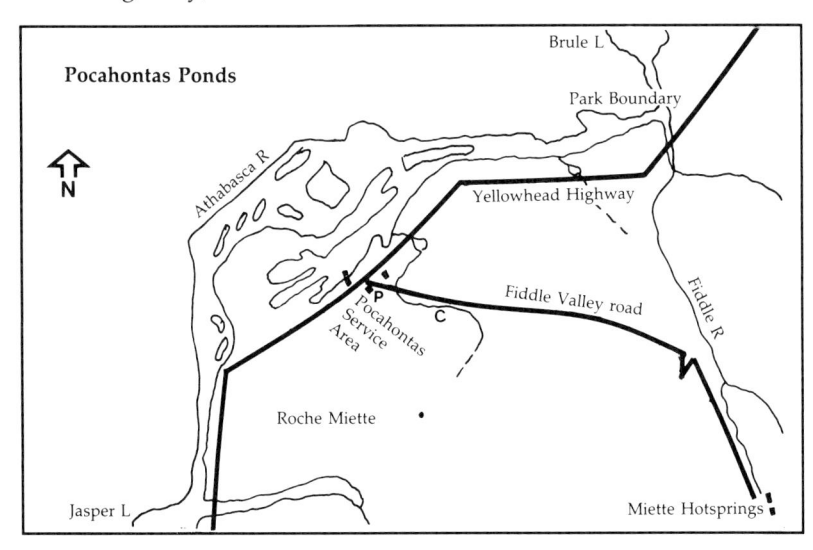

Habitat: Wetlands, flooded during much of the summer by overflow from the glacially-fed Athabasca River. Early and late in the season the water subsides, leaving small inter-connected ponds surrounded by extensive sedge meadows and willow thickets. Beware: this habitat is as good for mosquitos as it is for birds!

Birding: Always worth a stop, any time of the year.

Mid-April to late May: One of Jasper's most important waterfowl staging areas. Watch for tundra swan, Canada goose, three species of teal, and numerous other waterfowl and shorebirds.

Late May to mid-July: Many species nest in the shrubbery and sedge meadows, but annual flooding results in low densities of breeding waterfowl. This is the best spot in the park for such boreal rarities as magnolia warbler, ovenbird, white-throated sparrow and LeConte's sparrow - one of only two known nesting areas for the latter. Bald Eagles have nested near here. Other species regularly sighted are Barrow's goldeneye, rufous hummingbird, eastern kingbird, alder flycatcher, warbling vireo, Tennessee warbler, orange-crowned warbler, northern yellowthroat, savannah sparrow and Lincoln's sparrow.

Mid-July to late September: During the autumn migration this again becomes an important staging area for waterfowl and shorebirds. Watch for stilt sandpipers, as well as two kinds of yellowlegs. In August and September great blue herons are often seen. This is also a good area for migrating raptors.

3. TALBOT LAKE

Location: Along the southeast side of the Yellowhead Highway, from 25 to 31 km northeast of Jasper townsite (18 to 24 km west of the Jasper National Park east gate). There are several parking areas along the lake, and picnic areas at the south end as well as halfway along the lake. The most productive birding area is the north end.

Habitat: Moderately deep montane lake with extensive shallows at the north end. The north end is a complex of sedge beds, rushes, a few patches of cattail, and stretches of open, shallow water. White and black spruce forest adjoins the north end of the lake. The

Talbot Lake

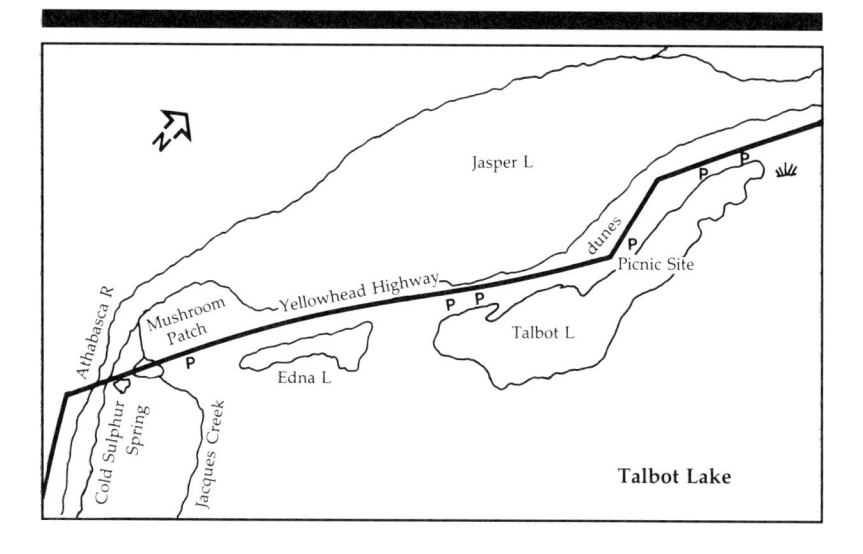

rest of the lake is surrounded by a mixture of dune grasslands and spruce forest. The dunes west of the highway are also worth exploring.

Birding: An important staging area for migrating coots and diving ducks.

Mid-April to late May: Concentrations of migrant waterfowl include Canada goose, red-necked and horned grebes, surf and white-winged scoters, hooded merganser, oldsquaw, Barrow's and common goldeneye, and bufflehead. Bald eagles, which formerly nested here, are regularly seen early in the spring.

Mid-May to mid-July: Canada goose families commonly graze right at the side of the road; Talbot Lake has one of the highest densities of nesting geese in the park. Watch the north end of the lake for such park rarities as marsh wrens and LeConte's sparrow. Ospreys nest across the narrows from the picnic site midway along the lake. Common loons nest on islands and beaver lodges at the north end of the lake.

Mid-July to late September: Diving ducks are more common than dabblers on fall migrations; sometimes large concentrations can be seen. Surf and white-winged scoter, hooded merganser, Barrow's and common goldeneyes and American coot are regularly seen. Bald eagles and other migrant raptors are seen from late August on.

4. MUSHROOM PATCH (Jacques Creek fan)

Location: Twenty km northeast of Jasper townsite (29 km from the Jasper east entrance) on both sides of the Yellowhead Highway. Parking available at the trailhead for Jacques and Merlin Passes. From there either wander along the hiking trail, or cross the highway and explore the willow thickets to the southwest.

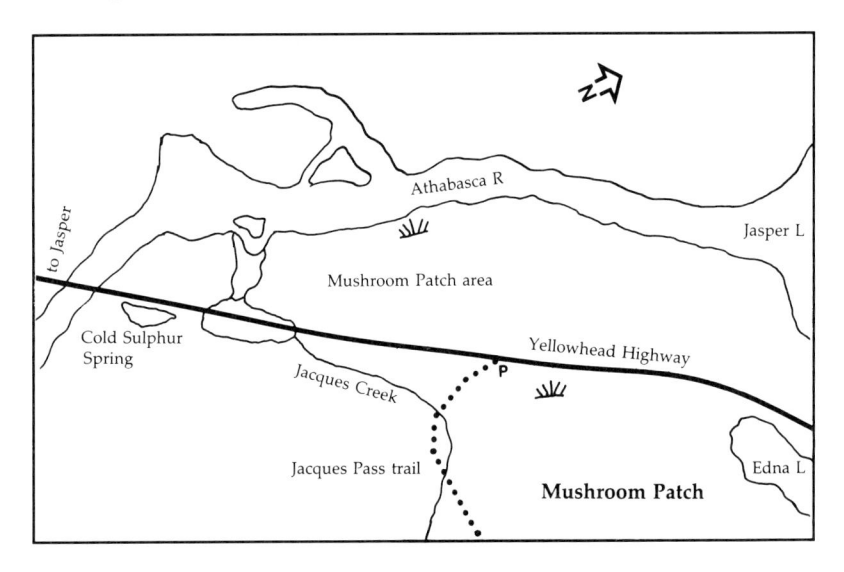

Habitat: Tall willow thickets with a tangled understory of nettles, raspberry canes and vetch. The surrounding forest is a mix of mature balsam poplar and white spruce. At the northwest end there is open grassland with clumps of snowberry and silverberry. This vegetation is fairly unique, probably because the location was once used for pasturing horses and the disturbance had long-lasting effects.

Birding: This is one of the most productive birding areas in the lower Athabasca valley, especially for small passerines. Beware of stinging nettles and be alert for bears.

> *Late April and early May:* Saw-whet and great horned owl may be heard calling at night and ruffed grouse can be heard drumming throughout the day. Check the old spruce woods for three-toed or pileated woodpecker, and watch the willows for downy and hairy woodpeckers, ruby-crowned kinglet and white-crowned sparrow.

Mid- and late May: Migrant warblers including orange-crowned, MacGillivray's, Tennessee and yellow, American redstart, red-eyed and warbling vireos, and chipping, clay-colored and white-throated sparrows are readily observed in the dense shrubbery.

June and early July: The Mushroom Patch supports an exceptional density of breeding passerines including all the above species. It is one of the best places in Jasper to see rufous hummingbird; several pairs breed here.

Winter: High densities of small rodents, particularly deer mouse and Gapper's red-backed vole, make this a likely area to look for northern shrike, great-horned owl, hawk owl and rough-legged hawk. Three-toed woodpecker and three chickadee species winter along the forest edges.

5. CELESTINE FIRE ROAD

Location: Joins highway 16 on its west side, 9.5 km north of Jasper townsite (39.5 km from the east gate). After crossing the upstream end of Snaring Lake and passing the Snaring Campground and Overflow, it becomes a narrow gravel road that winds for 30 km

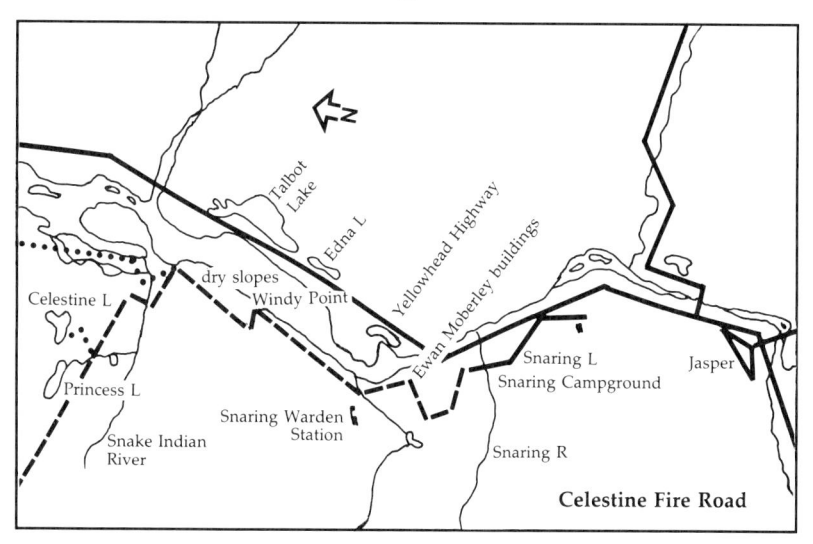

Celestine Fire Road

along the west side of the Athabasca valley and ends at the Celestine Lake parking lot. A gated extension forms the beginning of the famed North Boundary Trail. The road is closed in winter and is open the rest of the year for one-way traffic only, the direction depending on the time of day. Before exploring this fascinating but rugged little road, check at the Park Information Centre to find out about one-way times.

Habitat: Lodgepole pine forest, black spruce bog, dry white spruce forest, some beautiful stands of Douglas fir, and open grasslands. For part of its length the road traverses dry, grassy slopes overlooking Jasper Lake and the Athabasca River.

Birding: This is a big area, and the best sightings won't be made from the car. At any time of year it is worth while to explore the grassland and aspens near Snaring District Warden Station, the dry slopes above Windy Point, and the slopes above Jasper Lake.

Late April and early May: Saw-whet and pygmy owl may be heard calling at moonrise, especially near the Snaring Warden Station. Watch and listen for blue grouse and Townsend's solitaire, as well as flocks of Bohemian waxwing, at the forest edges above Jasper Lake.

June and early July: Park rarities such as Say's phoebe, Lewis' woodpecker, rock wren and prairie falcon have been sighted, especially near Windy Point. This is one of the driest areas in Jasper, so species more typical of the dry interior of British Columbia or the Alberta prairies occasionally show up here.

6. MALIGNE VALLEY ROAD

Location: Joins highway 16 just 1.5 km north of Jasper townsite and runs 48 km southeast up the Maligne River valley to Maligne Lake. It is a scenic day trip, crossing the head of Maligne Canyon and running along the length of Medicine Lake.

Habitat: Most of the lower valley was burned early in this century and is now covered with lodgepole pine and spruce forest. Maligne Canyon is a deep, shaded gorge abutted by open grassy slopes and pine forest. Medicine Lake almost disappears each fall, leaving extensive mudflats exposed. The Maligne River between Maligne and Medicine Lakes is clear, fast and fertile, and much of it remains unfrozen all winter.

Maligne Valley

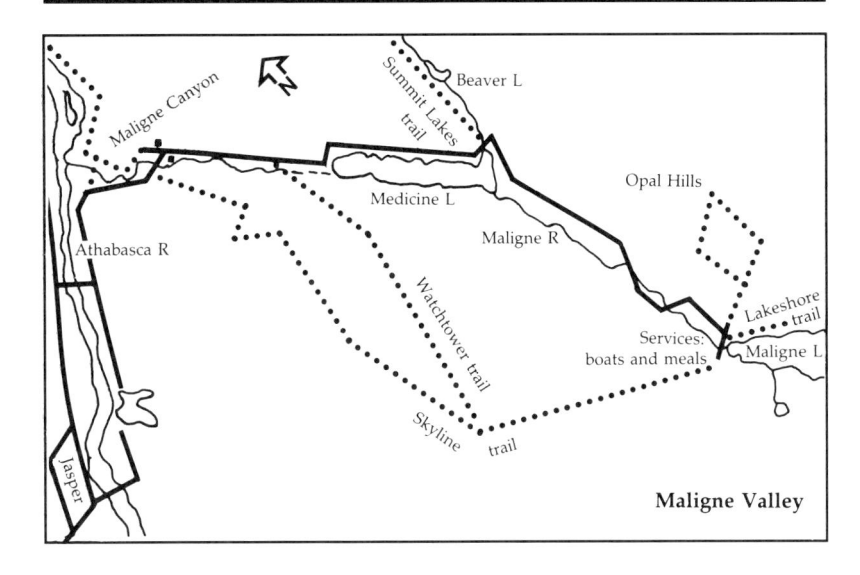

Birding: Like the Celestine Road, this is a day excursion by car which is most likely to produce good birding if you stop in one or two places to explore for a while.

April to early July: Raven nests may be observed in Maligne Canyon, and Townsend's solitaires nest on the open slopes above the canyon and along the road cut above Medicine Lake. One night I counted six different boreal owls calling near the outlet of Medicine Lake; listen for these here or along the Summit Lakes trail at the south end of Medicine, especially around moonrise in April and early May. Winter wren and varied thrush are common in the deep spruce woods at the lower end of Medicine Lake and along the Watchtower trail. Watch also for harlequin duck and American dipper all along the Maligne River, especially near where it leaves Maligne Lake.

Late June to early September: Black swifts nest at Maligne Canyon. This is one of only two or three breeding locations in Alberta. The swifts are most readily seen from the viewpoint north of the canyon at dusk as they return to the colony.

Late August and September: The mudflats along Medicine Lake attract migrating sandpipers, plovers and water pipits. Watch for bald eagles roosting in trees along the lake, as well as prairie falcons and other raptors hunting the lake edges.

7. COTTONWOOD SLOUGH

Location: Adjacent to the Pyramid Lake Road, 2 km west of Jasper townsite. Cottonwood Slough is the first pond on the left after leaving the townsite. There is parking on the south side of the pond, and a short trail along the south side. For a longer and more diverse walk, cross to the north side of the pond where a hiking and horse trail runs along the valley edge, linking with the Patricia Lake Circle trail. Current trail information and the free brochure *Day Hikes in Jasper National Park* are available at the Jasper townsite Information Centre.

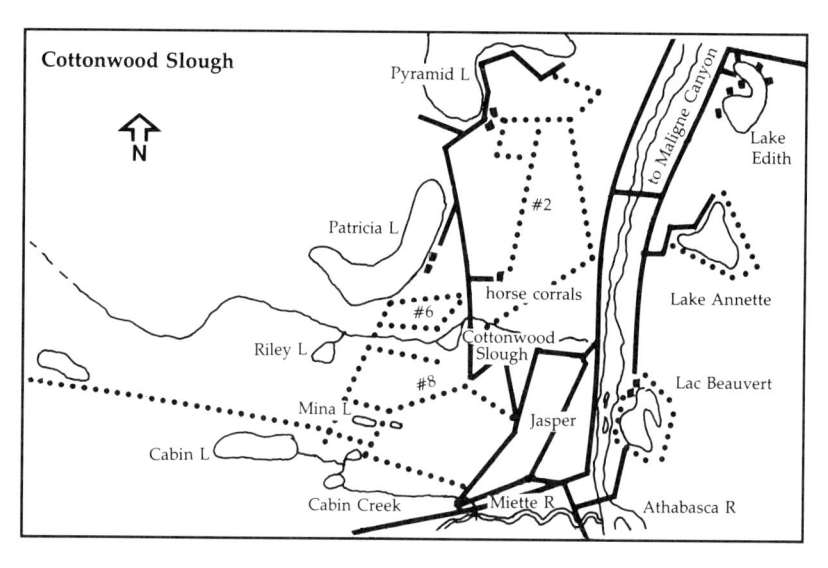

Habitat: A complex area - pine forest on north-facing slopes; grassland, aspen and Douglas fir groves on the southerly aspects; and a series of beaverponds, sedge meadows, black spruce bogs and willow thickets along the valley bottom.

Birding: If you have time for only one quick outing, this is the place to visit. Not only is it within walking distance of Jasper townsite, but it is one of the most productive birding areas in the park.

March to early May: Barred owl and pileated woodpecker both occur here. A moonlight stroll may also produce saw-whet, boreal or great horned owls, and will certainly produce common snipe beginning in April.

Late April to late May: Migrant and breeding waterfowl include pied-billed grebe, ring-necked duck and sora, species that are not often seen elsewhere in the park. Green-winged teal, bufflehead, Barrow's goldeneye, red-winged blackbird, song and Lincoln's sparrows, and the occasional swamp sparrow are also seen.

June and early July: Watch for ring-necked duck, Barrow's goldeneye, alder, willow, least and Hammond's flycatchers, northern waterthrush, orange-crowned warbler, northern yellowthroat, Wilson's warbler, rufous hummingbird, and clay-colored, song and Lincoln's sparrows. Several rare or unique sightings have been made here by local birders.

8. ATHABASCA RIVER

Location: Parallels highway 16 between the east park entrance and Jasper townsite, and highway 93 from the townsite south to

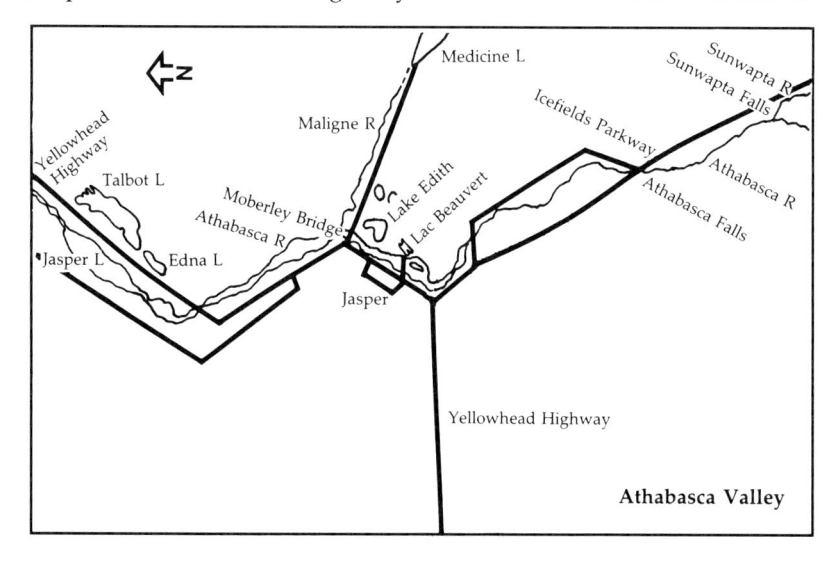

Sunwapta Falls. The most productive areas are the reach from just south of Jasper townsite (Old Fort Point) to the Mile 12 bridge (15 km northeast of the townsite), and the reach downstream from Jasper Lake to the park boundary.

Habitat: A typical glacial river, with numerous gravel bars and log jams. Water level fluctuates both during the day, and over the year, due to the influence of the glaciers that feed it. Rapids are more frequent upstream of Jasper townsite, while long smooth stretches are the rule downstream from the town. Most of the shoreline is forested with lodgepole pine or white spruce.

Birding:
Early May to early June: Watch for small groups of harlequin ducks on gravel bars and small islands near Jasper townsite and the mouth of the Maligne River. This is a major staging area for the species. Even if you miss the harlequins, you should see American dipper, spotted sandpiper, osprey and common merganser. There are osprey nests near the Moberley Bridge and downstream from Jasper Lake.
Mid-October to mid-May: American dippers remain all winter on stretches of open water along the river.

9. MIETTE VALLEY

Location: Adjacent to the Yellowhead Highway between Jasper townsite and the Jasper National Park west entrance at Yellowhead Pass. There are two areas of particular interest to birders: the mixed forest section from the Yellowhead Highway bridge across the Miette one km west of Jasper townsite, downstream to the confluence of the Athabasca River; and the wetlands from Decoigne Warden Station (one km east of the west park entrance) downstream to Geikie (14 km east of the west park entrance).

Habitat: The mixed forest section is an area of great vegetation diversity, with white spruce forest, balsam poplar stands, dense willow thickets, sedge meadows and even some Douglas fir forest. The best way to see the area is by canoe. The wetlands farther west are a mosaic of sedge meadows, shrub thickets, beaverponds, muskeg and spruce forest - another diverse and productive area, but considerably more open and accessible only to those who are willing to get their feet wet.

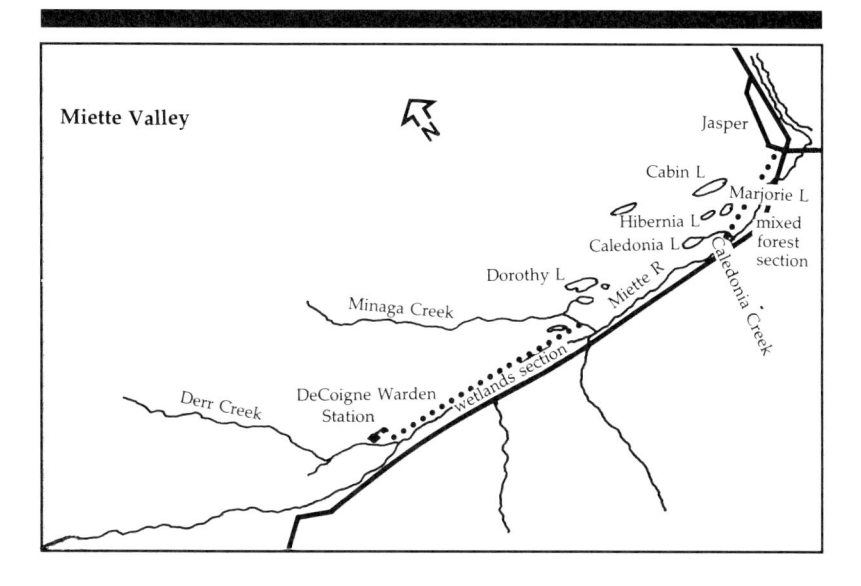

Birding: This, with Cottonwood Slough, is one of the most popular birding areas for local birders.

May through July: The mixed forest section is an ideal place for a short dawn or dusk canoe trip. Pileated woodpecker and barred owl nest here, rufous hummingbirds perform courtship flights along the river banks, and the canoeist can hear the songs of Tennessee, orange-crowned, yellow, yellow-rumped, blackpoll and Wilson's warblers, American redstart, warbling vireo, and purple finch. Many park rarities, including northern goshawk and Bullock's oriole have been sighted in this area.

The wetland section supports an abundance of nesting waterfowl, particularly Canada goose, mallard and green-winged teal. There are at least three osprey nests. This is a good area to watch for belted kingfisher and swallows, in addition to a variety of warblers, flycatchers and sparrows.

10. THE WHISTLERS and SIGNAL MOUNTAIN

Location: Both alpine areas are within easy reach of Jasper townsite. The Whistlers is reached by travelling 2 km south on the Icefields Parkway from its junction with the Yellowhead Highway, to the access road for the Jasper Tramway. Check at the Jasper townsite Information Centre for tramway hours of operation. It's by far the easiest way to get to the top of a mountain in Jasper.

Signal Mountain is less crowded and offers more productive birding. However, it is only for the birder who wants to earn his or her alpine list. To explore the Signal Mountain meadows, you must hike 6 km up the closed fire road that starts 5.5 km along the Maligne Road from its junction with the Yellowhead Highway.

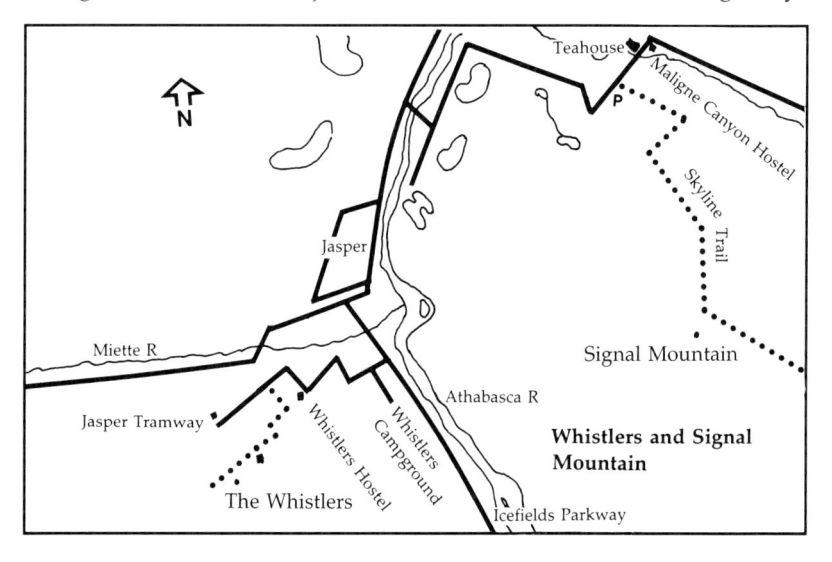

Habitat: Both mountains have extensive areas of alpine vegetation and rubble slopes. The Signal Mountain meadows are more lush and extensive, and there is the added bonus of open timberline forest along the Skyline Trail.

Birding:
Mid-June to late August: A half-day of hiking should produce a number of timberland and alpine specialties such as water pipit, Townsend's solitaire, horned lark, rosy finch, fox sparrow and white-tailed ptarmigan. Golden-crowned and Brewer's sparrows and, occasionally, willow ptarmigan may be found on Signal Mountain. During late August there is a possibility of seeing sharp-shinned hawk, northern harrier or prairie falcon migrating along the timberline ridges.

11. VALLEY OF FIVE LAKES

Location: Eight kilometres southeast of the Jasper townsite, in a narrow, glacially-gouged valley in the shadow of Signal Mountain. There are trailheads at Old Fort Point and beside the Icefields Parkway, 9 km south of its junction with the Yellowhead Highway. The lakes are only 3 or 4 km from the latter trailhead.

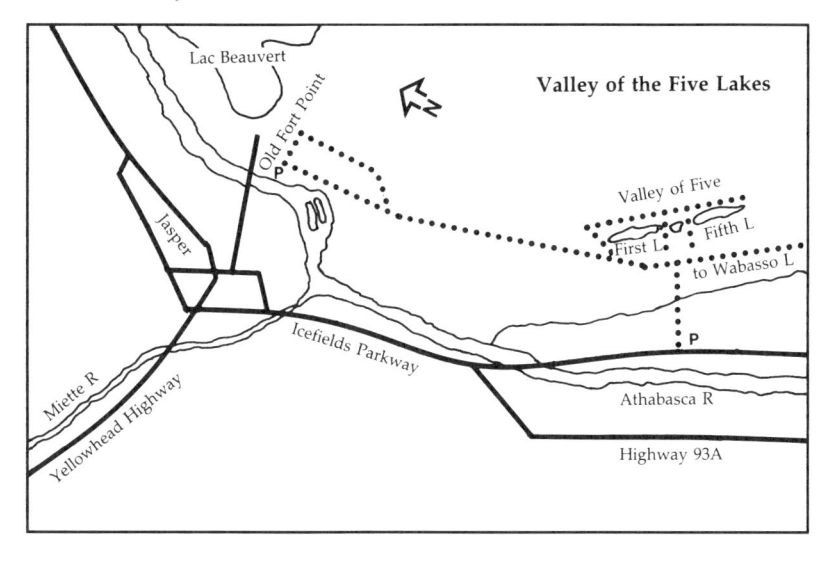

Habitat: A whole range of montane habitats - from lodgepole pine forest the trail drops into the Wabasso Creek valley and crosses a beaverpond complex before traversing a grassland slope onto a Douglas fir ridgetop. Then it drops through aspen and pine woods to the Valley of Five, where shrub and forest-bordered lakes are separated by grassy meadows and groves of pine.

Birding:
>*Mid-May to mid-July:* Common warblers include yellow-rumped, Tennessee, Townsend's, MacGillivray's and yellow warblers, northern yellowthroat and northern waterthrush. Other species include ruffed grouse, hermit thrush, Hammond's flycatcher and western tanager in the Douglas fir and mixed forest stands, Barrow's goldeneye, common loon and spotted sandpiper on the lakes, and occasional park rarities like grey catbird and clay-colored sparrow.

12. TONQUIN VALLEY - AMETHYST LAKES

Location: Justly renowned as one of the spectacular mountain landscapes that has made Jasper National Park famous for its beauty, the Tonquin Valley is accessible only on foot or horseback, with an overnight stay in a backcountry campground or one of two backcountry lodges. There are two trailheads south of Jasper townsite; enquire at the Jasper townsite Information Centre for details.

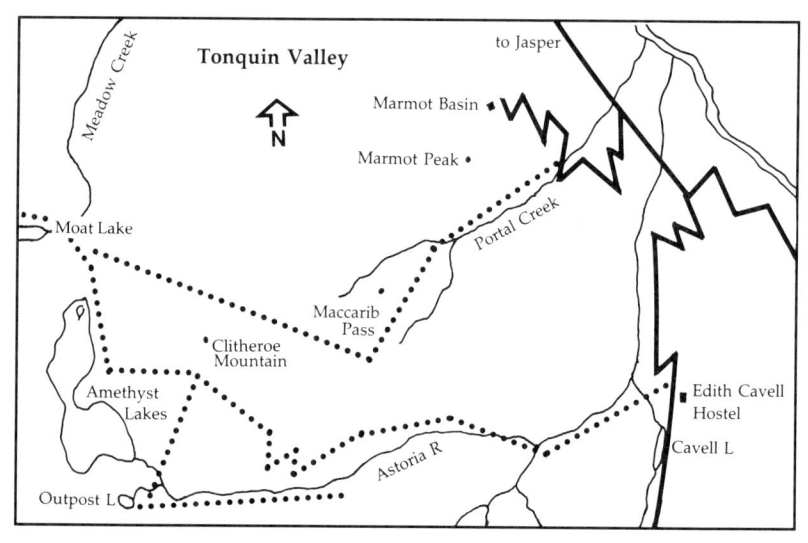

Habitat: Broad, high-elevation valley with large lakes and extensive sedge, willow and heather meadows flanked by a fringe of spruce/fir forest. Above, particularly on the flanks of Clitheroe and Maccarib Mountains, there are lush alpine meadows where caribou are often seen in summer.

Birding:
Mid-June to August: This area is an excellent place to search for willow ptarmigan, golden eagle and golden-crowned sparrow. Gray-cheeked thrushes have twice been found singing here during the breeding season.
Winter: Flocks of both willow and white-tailed ptarmigan can be found feeding in the willow meadows along Maccarib Creek and elsewhere in the area.

13. WILCOX PASS

Location: A day hike in the Columbia Icefield area at the south end of Jasper National Park, 107.5 km from Jasper townsite along the Icefields Parkway. There are trailheads at both Wilcox Creek and Columbia Icefield campgrounds.

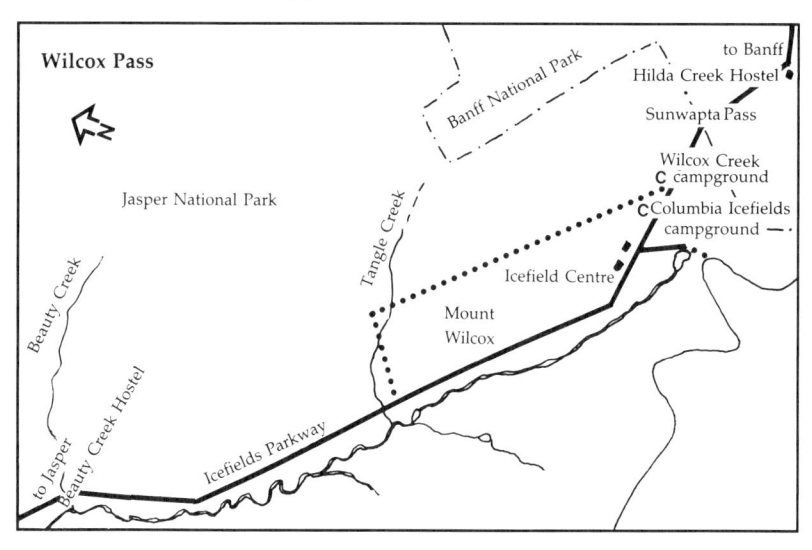

Habitat: After a short climb through spruce/fir forest (and some of the oldest trees in the park), the trail enters a broad alpine valley of heather meadows, wet sedge meadows, eroded gullies and talus slides.

Birding:
> *Mid-June to August:* White-tailed ptarmigan, horned lark, water pipit, Brewer's sparrow and golden eagle are seen regularly.
>
> *Mid-August to late September:* Watch for migrating raptors such as northern harrier, golden eagle, prairie falcon and the accipiters.

B. WINTER BIRDING IN JASPER NATIONAL PARK

During winter, as is the case just about anywhere in Canada and the northern U.S.A., the number and density of birds diminishes markedly. The most productive area is the Jasper townsite itself, since ornamental trees, bird feeders and warm buildings create an island of artificially-benign habitat in what may otherwise appear to be an inhospitable winter landscape. Among the species to look for around town are Steller's jay, black-billed magpie, raven, Clark's nutcracker, Bohemian waxwing, evening grosbeak, pine grosbeak and house sparrow. Pygmy owls have been recorded, rarely, on telephone lines and trees in town.

Boreal, mountain and black-capped chickadees and the ubiquitous gray jay are the species most likely to be seen elsewhere by the winter birder. Red-breasted nuthatches and golden-crowned kinglets are occasionally associated with flocks of chickadees. Both species of crossbills are usually present in winter. Willow and white-tailed ptarmigan winter along valley-bottom meadows at high elevations, such as Whistlers Creek, Portal Creek and the upper Maligne River.

The lower Athabasca River valley, between Jasper townsite and the east park entrance, has a number of small springs that result in open water all winter long. These are good places to look for over-wintering mallards and goldeneyes, as well as American dippers. The wind-blown landscape of the lower Athabasca is the best place to look for such winter rarities as northern shrike, rough-legged hawk, hawk owl, rosy finch and snow bunting.

Section IV. PLANNING A TRIP

Boreal Owl

Section IV. PLANNING A TRIP

Jasper National Park, like all of Canada's national parks, attracts visitors from all over the world. Birders who visit Jasper may be from Fredericton, Toronto, Vancouver, Whitehorse, California, Texas, London or Brisbane. It goes without saying that each birder has somewhat different interests than the others.

In order to help you tailor your trip to meet your personal birding objectives, the following offers suggestions as to what you might do with a half-day, a full day, or two or more days in Jasper National Park.

1. MOUNTAIN BIRD TOUR

Birds that are most sought after by birders visiting the Rocky Mountains for the first time may include Barrow's goldeneye, harlequin duck, golden eagle, white-tailed ptarmigan, pygmy owl, rufous hummingbird, Hammond's flycatcher, and other species that prefer alpine areas or the other characteristic habitats of Canada's Rockies.

Half day: Try a short walk at Cottonwood Slough (page 48) or along the Valley of Five Lakes trail (page 53).

If you are specifically interested in alpine species, take a stroll up the Wilcox Pass trail (page 55), or try the Jasper Tramway to the summit of The Whistlers (page 52), Another good place to explore is the Mount Edith Cavell meadows trail, a half-day hike in timberline country.

Full day: Drive up the Maligne River valley (page 46) stopping to explore the open slopes above Maligne Canyon, the Beaver Lake trailhead area, and the shoreline trail along Maligne Lake.

To add some alpine species to the day's list, try the Bald Hills or Opal Hills trails at Maligne Lake. They are both half-day hikes that should produce Brewer's and golden-crowned sparrow, water pipit and horned lark.

Another good full-day excursion is a drive to the Columbia Icefield area along Highway 93A and the Icefields Parkway. Stop at Leech Lake to look for waterfowl, watch for dippers along the Athabasca and Sunwapta Rivers, and spend a little time exploring the edge of the Beauty Creek flats. Then take half a day to hike up into Wilcox Pass (page 55).

Two or more days: For the backpacker, both the Tonquin Valley and Skyline trails offer a wide range of typical Rocky Mountain habitats and the opportunity to see most of the species associated with those habitats. Check at park information centres for free park use permits and backcountry information.

2. NORTHERN BIRD TOUR

Visitors from the United States and other areas are often interested in seeing the species that typify Canada's north. Because the Athabasca River valley drains northeast into the boreal vastness of northern Alberta, it is a natural corridor allowing boreal species to extend their ranges into the Rockies.

Half day: A drive or walk from Jasper townsite to Pyramid Lake, stopping to check waterbodies along the way, will produce such northern species as common loon, ring-necked duck, osprey, greater yellowlegs, alder flycatcher, boreal chickadee, Tennessee warbler and Lincoln's sparrow.

If you want to stretch your legs, explore the Cottonwood Slough area (page 48).

Full day: In addition to the half-day described above, consider a trip northeast along the Yellowhead Highway with stops at the Mushroom Patch (page 44) and Pocahontas Ponds (page 41). The magnolia warbler has been sighted in the spruce forest at the north end of Talbot Lake (page 42).

Two or more days: Camping at Pocahontas campground (page 40) is one way to improve the odds of finding bird species associated with the boreal vegetation that extends into the park around the east park entrance. Another northern bird found in Jasper National Park is the willow ptarmigan. Birders with a couple of days at their disposal may want to try to find this species; probably the best area to try is the Tonquin Valley and Maccarib Creek (page 54). An added lure of this area is that gray-cheeked thrushes have been found here in breeding season.

3. WESTERN BIRD TOUR

Besides the typical Rocky Mountain birds, Jasper National Park supports several species more typical of British Columbia than of Alberta, species that occur in only a few parts of the Rockies since they generally prefer habitats found farther west. For birders whose chief interest is in seeing blue grouse, pygmy owl, black swift, calliope hummingbird, dusky flycatcher, Steller's jay and Cassin's finch, the following trip ideas may help.

Half day: Try the Maligne Canyon area (page 46). Another good location for a short exploration is the Valley of Five Lakes trail (page 53).

Full day: The dry, open slopes along the Celestine Road (page 45) are well worth checking for western species. A full day will probably be necessary to allow you to explore on foot at a few places along the road, and perhaps hike in to Celestine or Princess Lakes at road-end.

Two or more days: While it is hard to improve on Maligne Canyon and the Celestine Road for a birder looking for western species, you may find it worthwhile to spend some time exploring the Miette valley (page 50), west of Jasper townsite. Near the mouths of Meadow and Clairvaux Creeks there is a possibility of finding Steller's jay and other species that are typical of the lush forests on the rainy western side of the Rockies.

4. BIG LIST BIRD TOUR

Let's face it, most birders who deny being listers are only fooling themselves. The competitive aspect of birding is one of its attractions. The beauty of listing is that you can compete against yourself.

For those who want to take a shot at finding 100 species in a single day in Jasper National Park, here are some suggestions. But if you get your hundred, you'll have earned them; the Rocky Mountain environment is not a productive one, and bird diversity is scattered over a few, often isolated, patches of habitat.

Half day: If you have time to explore only one area, make it Cottonwood Slough (page 48). Not only is there a variety of habitats, but several of the ones here are among our most productive. In addition, the area is right at the junction of three major valleys, so it's a likely spot for any migrants or wanderers that are funnelling through the Rockies.

Full day: Check Cottonwood Slough, then glass for waterfowl on Patricia and Pyramid Lakes. A short drive northeast along the Yellowhead Highway will take you to the Mushroom Patch (page 44) and Pocahontas Ponds (page 41) and then, if you want to make a long day of it, you can add a few more species to your list by taking an evening canoe trip or stroll along the lower Miette River (page 50).

Two or more days: The options really increase as the available time increases. The main thing to consider is that the most productive habitats, and thus the highest diversity of birds, are along the low-elevation valley bottoms. So it pays to concentrate on the areas already listed. In addition, you may want to check Lakes Edith and Annette, Mildred Lake and Talbot Lake (page 42). The wetlands along the Miette River (page 50) near the west park entrance are worth a ramble. In addition, the Mount Edith Cavell meadows or The Whistlers (page 52) offer half-day opportunities to add timberline and alpine species to your list.

5. RARITIES AND UNIQUE SPECIES BIRD TOUR

The attraction of finding something totally unexpected is always at the back of a birder's mind when he or she sets out into the field. Jasper National Park offers both the chance to find rare species with relative ease, if you know where to look, in addition to the possibility of tripping over something you never dreamed of seeing. In May, 1988, for example, a Bendire's thrasher spent four days in the park where it was observed and photographed by several incredulous birders.

The best seasons for finding the unexpected are late May/early June, and August/early September. During the former period, spring migration is almost over and birds are highly vocal and detectable. Some migrating stragglers are likely to be still trying to find their ways through the Rockies, especially if there have been violent spring storms to the west or east. During the latter period, fall migration is beginning, and many non-breeding individuals or early migrants are wandering about, often turning up far from their normal ranges.

But any time of year is good. Here are some specific suggestions for some of Jasper's rare or unique species:

Red-necked Grebe:	Pyramid, Patricia and Mildred Lakes
Pied-billed Grebe:	Cottonwood Slough and Pocahontas Ponds
Golden Eagle:	Wilcox Pass and Tonquin Valley
Bald Eagle:	Pocahontas Ponds area and Medicine Lake
Willow Ptarmigan:	Maccarib Creek and Signal Mountain
Pygmy Owl:	Celestine Road
Barred Owl:	Cottonwood Slough and lower Miette River
Boreal Owl:	Medicine Lake and Summit Lakes
Black Swift:	Maligne Canyon
Pileated Woodpecker:	Cottonwood Slough and lower Miette River
Three-toed Woodpecker:	Lower Miette River and Summit Lakes
Cliff Swallow:	Maligne Lake and Yellowhead Highway bridges
Marsh Wren:	North end of Talbot Lake
Rock Wren:	Celestine Road (Windy Point) and Medicine Lake
Gray-cheeked Thrush:	Tonquin Valley
Veery:	Pocahontas Ponds
Magnolia Warbler:	Talbot Lake
Palm Warbler:	Sunwapta Falls
Ovenbird:	Mushroom Patch and Pocahontas Ponds

Cassin's Finch: Pyramid Lake
LeConte's Sparrow: Pocahontas Ponds
Brewer's Sparrow: Wilcox Pass and Opal Hills
White-throated Sparrow: Pocahontas Ponds and Mushroom Patch
Swamp Sparrow: Cottonwood Slough

One of the most interesting, and unusual, day trips for a birder interested in the chance of seeing something unique and unexpected, is the drive along the Celestine Road (page 45) to Celestine and Princess Lakes. Another idea is to check the larger lakes and ponds along the Athabasca valley, particularly Pyramid, Patricia, Mildred and Talbot Lakes (page 42). Unusual migrant shorebirds, as well as bald eagles and other raptors, turn up in late July and August along Medicine (page 46) and Jasper Lakes and in the Pocahontas Ponds (page 41).

But rarities are where you find them. The attraction of looking for them in Jasper National Park is that there are few more attractive and fascinating places in the world to search. Good luck!

AFTERWORD

For further specific information, or to check on recent sightings or current conditions in the Park, please drop in at the Jasper townsite Information Centre or the Icefield Centre. You can also write or telephone the Jasper National Park Interpretive Service at the following address:

Superintendent
Jasper National Park
Box 10
Jasper, Alberta
T0E 1E0
Attention: Chief Park Interpreter

Phone: (403) 852-6176

SELECTED BIBLIOGRAPHY

Gadd, B.,1986. *Handbook of the Canadian Rockies*.
       Corax Press, Jasper.

Patton, B.,1982. *Parkways of the Canadian Rockies*.
       Summerthought Publishing, Banff.

Patton, B. and B. Robinson,1986. *Canadian Rockies Trail Guide*.
       Summerthought Publishing, Banff.

Salt, W.R. and J.R.,1976. *Birds of Alberta*.
       Hurtig Publishers, Edmonton.

Canadian Parks Service, *Day Hikes in Jasper National Park*,
       free brochure, available at park information centres.

GENERAL INDEX

Accipiters	56
Alder	25, 41
Alpine	11, 24, 28, 52, 53, 54, 55, 58, 61
Aspen	11, 18, 19, 20, 21, 40, 46, 48, 53
Athabasca Glacier	23
Athabasca valley	11, 12, 16, 19, 44, 46, 56, 63
Avalanche slope	4, 25, 26, 27
Backcountry	54
Bald Hills	58
Balsam poplar	18, 19, 21, 40, 41, 44, 50
Banff National Park	11, 15
Bear	44
Bearberry	17, 18
Beauty Creek flats	59
Beaver	27, 43
Beaverpond	13, 14, 48, 50, 53
Bighorn Dam	16
Bighorn sheep	16, 17
Black spruce	11, 14, 18, 21, 42, 46, 48
Blackbird, red-winged	14, 49
Bluebird, mountain	16, 24
Boreal	11, 40, 42, 59
Bridgland	19
Buffaloberry	18
Bufflehead	43, 49
Bunting, snow	56
Burn	10
Canoe	50, 51
Caribou	54
Catbird, grey	54
Cattail	42
Cavell meadows	23, 24, 28, 58, 61
Celestine Road	17, 21, 60, 63
Checklist	30
Chickadee, black-capped	45, 56
Chickadee, boreal	18, 23, 45, 56, 59
Chickadee, mountain	15, 45, 56
Clairvaux Creek	60
Columbia Icefield area	22, 55, 59

Coot, American 43
Cottonwood Slough 13, 14, 21, 22, 48, 51, 58, 59, 61
Creek, Cottonwood 13
Creek, Wabasso. 13, 14
Crossbill, red 56
Crossbill, white-winged. 56
Currant 25
Day Hikes in Jasper National Park 48
Decoigne Warden Station 50
Deer mouse 45
Dipper, American 27, 47, 50, 56
Disaster Point. 17
Diving ducks 43
Douglas fir 11, 15, 17, 46, 48, 50, 53, 54
Dry slopes. 16
Duck, harlequin. 27, 47, 50, 58
Duck, ring-necked. 13, 49, 59
Dunes. 43
Dwarf birch. 21, 26
Eagle, bald 42, 43, 47, 62, 63
Eagle, golden 25, 27, 55, 56, 58, 62
Elk. 16, 25
Engelmann spruce 10
Falcon, prairie 4, 5, 46, 47, 53, 56
Fiddle Valley 40
Finch, Cassin's. 15, 60, 63
Finch, purple 21, 51
Finch, rosy 10, 28, 53, 56
Flicker, northern 5, 15, 19, 24
Flicker, red-shafted. 19
Flicker, yellow-shafted. 19
Flycatcher, alder 14, 21, 27, 42, 49, 59
Flycatcher, dusky 60
Flycatcher, Hammond's. 10, 18, 21, 23, 26, 41, 49, 54, 58
Flycatcher, least. 21, 41, 49
Flycatcher, olive-sided. 21, 26
Flycatcher, willow. 14, 49
Geikie. 50
Goldeneye, Barrow's 13, 42, 43, 49, 54, 58
Goldeneye, common 43, 56
Goose, Canada. 42, 43, 51
Goshawk, northern. 17, 51

Grass 24, 25, 26
Grassland 11, 14, 15, 43, 44, 46, 48, 53
Gravel bar 50
Grebe, horned 43
Grebe, pied-billed 49, 62
Grebe, red-necked 13, 43, 62
Grizzly bear 25
Grosbeak, evening 56
Grosbeak, pine 25, 56
Ground squirrel, Columbian 25
Ground squirrel, golden-mantled 17
Grouse, blue 17, 46, 60
Grouse, ruffed 21, 44, 54
Grouse, spruce 21
Harrier, northern 27, 53, 56
Hawk, red-tailed 21
Hawk, rough-legged 45, 56
Hawk, sharp-shinned 53
Heath 24
Heather 24, 54, 55
Heron, great blue 42
Huckleberry 25
Hummingbird, calliope 17, 60
Hummingbird, rufous 14, 19, 24, 41, 42, 45, 49, 51, 58
Icefields Parkway 52, 53, 55
Jacques Creek 44
Jacques Pass 44
Jaeger, parasitic 12
Jasper townsite 5, 13, 16, 17, 19, 48, 49, 50, 56, 59
Jasper Tramway 52, 58
Jasper/Banff boundary 27
Jay, blue 5
Jay, gray 18, 56
Jay, Steller's 5, 11, 56, 60
Junco, dark-eyed 5, 21, 23
Junco, Oregon 23
Juniper 18
Kestrel, American 15, 16, 17
Kettle pond 13
Kingbird, eastern 42
Kingbird, western 12
Kingfisher, belted 51

Kinglet, golden-crowned 23, 56
Kinglet, ruby-crowned 14, 21, 24, 44
Kittiwake, black-legged 12
Kootenay Plains 15
Krummholz 24
Labrador tea 21
Lake, Annette 13, 61
Lake, Beaver 58
Lake, Cabin 13
Lake, Celestine 46, 60, 63
Lake, Edith 13, 61
Lake, Geraldine 26
Lake, Honeymoon 22
Lake, Jasper 46, 50, 63
Lake, Leech 59
Lake, Maligne 27, 46, 47, 58
Lake, Medicine 46, 47, 63
Lake, Mildred 13, 61, 63
Lake, Patricia 13, 21, 61, 63
Lake, Princess 60, 63
Lake, Pyramid 13, 21, 59, 61, 63
Lake, Riley 22
Lake, Snaring 45
Lake, Summit 47
Lake, Talbot 13, 22, 43, 59, 61, 63
Lakes 12, 14
Lark, horned 28, 53, 56, 58
Listing 60
Little Ice Age 10
Lodgepole pine 10, 17, 40, 46, 50, 53
Log jam 50
Loon, common 13, 43, 54, 59
Maccarib Creek 55, 60
Maccarib Mtn 54
Maccarib Pass 28
Magpie, black-billed 56
Main Ranges 10
Maligne Canyon 46, 47, 58, 60
Maligne River 46, 47, 50, 56
Maligne Road 52
Maligne Valley 58
Mallard 13, 51, 56

Marmot, hoary 25
Meadow Creek 60
Meadowlark, western 16
Medicine Lake 4
Menziesia 23
Merganser, common 50
Merganser, hooded 43
Merlin 5
Merlin Pass 44
Miette valley 11, 12, 18, 19, 60
Mile 12 bridge 50
Milton and Cheadle 21
Mixed forest 18, 41, 50, 54
Moberley Bridge 50
Montane 11, 40, 42, 53
Moose 21, 25
Mosquito 21, 22, 42
Moss 21, 23
Mt. Clitheroe 54
Mudflats 4, 46, 47
Mule deer 17
Mushroom Patch 14, 18, 59, 61
Muskeg 21, 22, 50
National Parks Act 17
Nettle 44
Nighthawk, common 16
North Boundary Trail 46
Nutcracker, Clark's 4, 17, 23, 24, 56
Nuthatch, red-breasted 15, 23, 26, 56
Old Fort Point 50, 53
Oldest trees 55
Oldsquaw 43
Opal Hills 27, 58
Oriole, Bullock's 51
Oriole, northern 5, 51
Osprey 13, 43, 50, 51, 59
Ovenbird 11, 41, 42, 62
Owl, barred 19, 49, 51, 62
Owl, boreal 5, 19, 26, 47, 49, 62
Owl, great horned 44, 45, 49
Owl, hawk 45, 56
Owl, pygmy 5, 15, 17, 19, 46, 56, 58, 60, 62

Owl, saw-whet 19, 21, 44, 46, 49
Patricia Lake Circle trail 48
Peat 21
Phoebe, Say's 11, 17, 46
Pine forest 17, 48
Pipit, water 10, 24, 28, 47, 53, 56, 58
Plovers 47
Pocahontas 40, 41
Pocahontas campground 59
Pocahontas ponds 13, 14, 59, 61, 63
Ponds 12, 14
Poplar 14
Portal Creek 56
Portal Creek trail 26
Ptarmigan, white-tailed 10, 28, 53, 55, 56, 58
Ptarmigan, willow 4, 5, 11, 25, 53, 55, 56, 60, 62
Pyramid bench 13, 14
Pyramid Lake Road 48
Raptors 42, 43, 47, 56, 63
Raspberry 44
Raven, common 47, 56
Red-backed vole 45
Redstart, American 45, 51
Rhododendron 23
River, Athabasca 10, 11, 13, 19, 42, 46, 56, 59
River, Brazeau 10
River, Miette 13, 19, 61
River, North Saskatchewan 10, 15
River, Smoky 10
Rivers 14
Robin, American 18, 24
Rush 42
Ryegrass 18
Sandpiper, Baird's 11
Sandpiper, semipalmated 4
Sandpiper, spotted 27, 50, 54
Sandpiper, stilt 42
Sandpipers 47
Sapsucker, red-naped 21
Scaup, lesser 13
Schaffer, Mary 21
Scoter 13

Scoter, surf 43
Scoter, white-winged 43
Sedge 14, 18, 21, 26, 42, 48, 50, 54, 55
Sedge/willow 14
Shintangle 24
Shorebirds 42, 63
Shrike, northern 45, 56
Shrubby meadows 26
Signal Mountain 4, 28, 52, 53
Silverberry 44
Siskin, pine 21
Skyline Trail 24, 27, 52, 59
Snaring Campground 45
Snaring District Warden Station 46
Snipe, common 14, 21, 27, 49
Snowberry 44
Solitaire, Townsend's 17, 24, 46, 47, 53
Sora 49
Sparrow, Brewer's 25, 53, 56, 58, 63
Sparrow, chipping 17, 18, 21, 45
Sparrow, clay-colored 41, 45, 49, 54
Sparrow, fox 25, 53
Sparrow, golden-crowned 5, 11, 25, 53, 55, 58
Sparrow, Harris' 5
Sparrow, house 56
Sparrow, Leconte's 11, 42, 43, 63
Sparrow, Lincoln's 14, 21, 26, 42, 49, 59
Sparrow, savannah 21, 27, 42
Sparrow, song 14, 49
Sparrow, swamp 12, 49, 63
Sparrow, vesper 16
Sparrow, white-crowned 5, 10, 25, 44
Sparrow, white-throated 5, 11, 41, 42, 45, 63
Sphagnum 21
Spruce forest 41
Spruce/fir forest 22, 26, 54, 55
Starling, European 16
Streams 14
Subalpine fir 4, 10, 25
Sulphur Skyline 17
Summit Lakes 47
Sunwapta District Warden Station 22

71

Sunwapta Falls... 50
Sunwapta Pass... 27
Sunwapta River.. 59
Swallow, barn 27
Swallow, cliff 62
Swallow, tree 14
Swallow, violet-green...................................... 14
Swallows... 51
Swan, tundra 42
Swift, black... 47, 60, 62
Talus...28, 55
Tamarack.. 11
Tanager, western.................................. 15, 19, 54
Teal.. 13
Teal, blue-winged 42
Teal, cinnamon 42
Teal, green-winged................................. 42, 49, 51
The Whistlers......................... 23, 26, 28, 52, 58, 61
Thrush, gray-cheeked 11, 55, 60, 62
Thrush, hermit...................................... 21, 23, 54
Thrush, Swainson's 18, 23
Thrush, varied..................................... 23, 24, 47
Timberline.................... 11, 24, 26, 27, 28, 52, 53, 58, 61
Tonquin Valley 23, 26, 27, 28, 54, 59, 60
Turnstone, ruddy 4
Valley of Five lakes............................... 14, 58, 60
Veery 62
Vetch 44
Vireo, red-eyed 45
Vireo, solitary..18, 41
Vireo, warbling 21, 41, 42, 45, 51
Wabasso Creek 53
Warbler, Audubon's.. 10
Warbler, blackpoll................................. 21, 41, 51
Warbler, MacGillivray's............................ 26, 45, 54
Warbler, magnolia................................. 21, 42, 59, 62
Warbler, orange-crowned 21, 42, 45, 49, 51
Warbler, palm 21, 62
Warbler, Tennessee 14, 19, 41, 42, 45, 51, 54, 59
Warbler, Townsend's............................... 23, 26, 54
Warbler, Wilson's 14, 19, 23, 25, 49, 51
Warbler, yellow 14, 45, 51, 54

Warbler, yellow-rumped 5, 45, 51, 54
Watchtower trail 23, 47
Waterfowl 42, 49, 51
Waterthrush, northern.................................. 49, 54
Waxwing, Bohemian 27, 46, 56
Wetland... 61
Wetlands.. 14, 50
Whistlers Creek 56
White spruce 17, 18, 19, 40, 42, 44, 46, 50
Wilcox Creek 55
Wilcox Pass.................................... 24, 28, 58, 59
Willow 14, 18, 24, 25, 26, 42, 44, 48, 50, 54, 55
Windy Point... 46
Winter 56
Wood-pewee, western 21
Woodpecker, downy 19, 44
Woodpecker, hairy 19, 44
Woodpecker, Lewis'........................... 11, 15, 17, 46
Woodpecker, pileated 15, 19, 44, 49, 51, 62
Woodpecker, three-toed 19, 26, 44, 45, 62
Wren, marsh 43, 62
Wren, rock 5, 11, 17, 46, 62
Wren, winter 23, 47
Yellowhead highway 17
Yellowhead Pass 11, 50
Yellowlegs, greater 11, 42, 59
Yellowlegs, lesser 42
Yellowthroat, northern 14, 42, 49, 54

Parks and People

73